INSECTS & BUGS

BACKYARD WORKBOOK

Hands-on Projects, Quizzes, and Activities For Kids

Jaret C. Daniels, PhD

Acknowledgments

I would like to thank my loving wife and best friend, Stephanie, for her unending patience, sense of humor, and support. She makes our life together truly wonderful. I also want to thank our many doting cats. They regularly keep me company during projects like this and quickly alert me should any of the assorted insects in our home escape. Lastly, I wish to thank my parents for encouraging my early interest in the natural world. It resulted in a continuously rewarding and always surprising career.

10 9 8 7 6 5 4 3 2

Edited by Brett Ortler
Cover and book design by Fallon Venable
Photo Credits on pages 118–119

Insects & Bugs Backyard Workbook: Hands-on Projects, Quizzes, and Activities for Kids
Copyright © 2021 by Jaret C. Daniels, PhD
Published by Adventure Publications, an imprint of AdventureKEEN
310 Garfield Street South, Cambridge, Minnesota 55008
(800) 678-7006
www.adventurepublications.net
ISBN 978-1-64755-159-9 (pbk.)

Safety Note

Learning about bugs and insects is a lot of fun, but whether you're in your back yard or at the beach, you always want to stay safe.

Follow these guidelines:
- Never go out alone! Always bring an adult.
- If you're venturing far, bring a map, a smart phone, or a GPS so that you don't get lost.
- Always bring water to drink. It's dangerous to be out all day with no water!
- Bring a hat and wear long clothes to protect you from the sun. You may get hot, but at least you won't get burned!
- Wear insect repellent to protect you from mosquitoes, ticks, no-see-ums (biting midges), and chiggers.
- Never go into rivers, lakes, or oceans because the water may be deeper or faster than you realize.
- Never go onto private property. This means that someone else owns the land. If you see signs that say "no trespassing," turn around right away!
- Always carry a flashlight if going outside at night.
- Avoid handling bugs. Many can bite, sting, pinch, or otherwise cause irritation. This is particularly true with bees, wasps, ants, centipedes, and scorpions. If you or someone in your family is allergic to stings and bites, don't closely approach insects and always be aware of your surroundings.
- Use caution when turning over logs, rocks, or other objects, or when reaching into cavities or crevices, and wear gloves if you plan to do so.
- Some bugs have irritating hairs or secretions. Always wash your hands after collecting.

Table of Contents

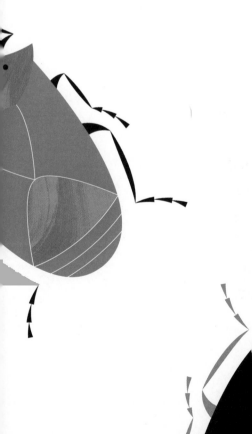

Amazing Insects

Insects are amazing. They are easy to find in almost any outdoor space. They come in an incredible variety of different sizes, shapes, and colors, and they can be both creepy and attractive. In fact, about 1 million different insect species are known to exist, making them the most diverse group of animals on Earth. Insects are also super abundant. This means that if you tried to count all the insects on the planet, you would end up with a really, really, really big number.

Fast Fact

At any one time, scientists estimate that there are some 10 quintillion (1,000,000,000,000,000,000) insects around—or about 200 million insects for every single person. That's a lot of insects!

What is an Insect?

Now, if you want to find, observe, or study insects, it helps to know what an insect is. For starters, insects are often called bugs. When you use the word "bug" you probably are referring to a range of small, creepy-crawly critters such as spiders, centipedes, millipedes, and scorpions, as well as insects. All of those small organisms belong to a large group called arthropods. Arthropods have an external skeleton (called an exoskeleton), a segmented body, and jointed appendages such as legs and antennae. There are several different groups of arthropods: hexapods (insects and springtails), crustaceans, arachnids (spiders and ticks), and myriapods (millipedes and centipedes).

Insects are by far the most well-known and commonly seen arthropods. They are also the largest group of arthropods.

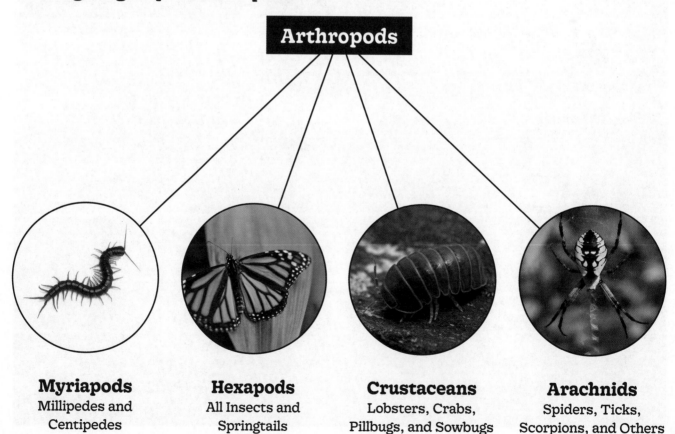

Arthropods

Myriapods
Millipedes and Centipedes

Hexapods
All Insects and Springtails

Crustaceans
Lobsters, Crabs, Pillbugs, and Sowbugs

Arachnids
Spiders, Ticks, Scorpions, and Others

Fast Fact

If you picked out any one living thing on Earth at random, there's a very good chance that it'd be an insect.

Insect Anatomy

All insects share the same basic body plan, with three main body sections: the head, thorax, and abdomen, as well as six legs and two antennae. The **head** is the first body section. It has two compound eyes, two antennae, and mouthparts. The **compound eyes** are used for seeing. They are composed of hundreds of smaller individual eyes. Above the eyes are two segmented **antennae**. They are used for sensing touch, taste, or smell. Insect antennae come in many different shapes. The head also has **mouthparts** used primarily for feeding. They are most commonly used for chewing or sucking, and the type of mouthparts vary between insects. Some adult insects lack mouthparts altogether and don't eat. As adults, they survive on stored food and only live to reproduce.

Diagram of Insect Anatomy

1. Head	2. Thorax	3. Abdomen	4. Antennae
5. Compound Eye	6. Foreleg	7. Middle Leg	8. Hind Leg
9. Forewing	10. Hindwing		

Examples from the Insect World:

A Tiger Beetle's head with jaws

A Wheel Bug's beak

A fly's sponging mouthparts

Real-World Diagram of Insect Anatomy

1. Head
2. Thorax
3. Abdomen
4. Antennae
5. Compound Eye
6. Legs
7. Forewing
8. Hindwing

The **thorax** is the second body section. It has six legs attached, two on each of the three segments. The **legs** enable an insect to move. They may also be used for other tasks such as digging, jumping, and capturing or holding prey. The leg has several parts. These include the femur, tibia, tarsus, and a tarsal claw. Many adult insects may also have **wings;** some, like flies, have two wings, while others, such as beetles and bees, have four. Wings are used for flying.

Examples from the Insect World:

An Eastern Lubber Grasshopper's thorax

Close-up of the legs and feet of a Western Honeybee

Close-up of a damselfly's wings

The final body section is the **abdomen**. It is also the longest and has the most segments. The abdomen has a series of small holes on the side, one pair on each segment, called **spiracles**. They are used for breathing. While also found on the thorax, they are most noticeable on the abdomen.

Examples from the Insect World:

Spiracles on a Tomato Hornworm caterpillar

Close-up of a German Yellowjacket's stinger and abdomen

A Goldenrod Soldier Beetle's abdomen

Activity: Label the Parts of this House Fly

Label the head, thorax, legs, abdomen, and compound eyes.

1.

2.

3.

4.

5.

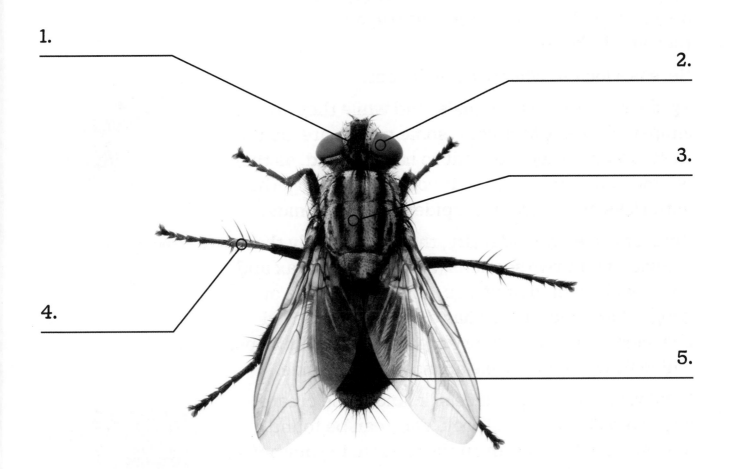

Quiz Time

1. How many wings does a house fly have?

_____

2. How many wings does a butterfly have?

_____

Answers on page 105! ☞

What's *Not* an Insect?

Many arthropods, such as spiders, millipedes, centipedes, and sowbugs and pillbugs, are often lumped together with insects, but they are different.

Here is a look at what's *not* an insect.

Spiders are familiar animals, and while they are almost all totally harmless, some people are afraid of them. In fact, they are great to have around, as they eat mosquitoes and other annoying bugs. Together with ticks and scorpions, spiders are arachnids.

Spiders are easy to identify; they have a body that is divided into two sections (the cephalothorax and abdomen), eight jointed legs, and no antennae or wings. Their mouth also has a pair of jaws called chelicerae and two sensory organs called pedipalps, which function much like an insect's antennae.

Finally, all spiders produce silk, and some create large webs for catching prey. They can be found almost anywhere, from on the ground, in your house or garage, under logs or rocks, and, if you look close, even hiding in plants or on flowers.

Millipedes are shiny, often dark colored, worm-like creatures. They have a long, and somewhat hardened, tube-like body with many visible segments. Most segments have two pairs of small, jointed legs. While the name millipede means "thousand legs," millipedes only have up to a few hundred legs, and they crawl slowly across the ground. If disturbed, many millipedes curl up into a spiral.

Zebra Jumping Spider

Warning: While most spiders prefer to hide or run away from people, many spiders can bite, so don't handle them.

Black Yellow Garden Spider

Despite their strange appearance, millipedes are completely harmless. Most millipedes are scavengers and feed on dead leaves and decaying plants and wood. They are most often found in dark, damp locations such as under logs, rocks, mulch, or even in flowerpots.

Centipedes look similar to millipedes but have a noticeably flattened body. They have only one pair of jointed legs on each segment; these legs extend outward from the side of the body. Unlike millipedes, centipedes can move quickly, especially if disturbed, often scurrying in a snake-like motion.

They are ferocious predators and active primarily at night. During the day, they can be found in dark, damp places such as under logs, rock, mulch or leaves.

Earthworms have long, tube-like segmented bodies, but unlike insects or other arthropods, they don't have an exoskeleton or any jointed legs. They instead have a fluid-filled body cavity surrounded by muscle. A combination of fluid pressure and muscle action keeps the earthworm's body shape and enables it to move.

They require moist environments, and are commonly found in soil, under leaf litter, rocks or logs. Earthworms are very beneficial decomposers, feeding on decaying plant material, small microorganisms, fungi and animal waste. While they may be slimy, earthworms are completely harmless.

A Millipede and a Centipede

Warning: Don't touch or hold centipedes, as they can deliver a painful bite.

Earthworm

What's *Not* an Insect?

Sowbugs and **Pillbugs** are weird-looking organisms that resemble tiny armadillos. They aren't insects, or even arthropods at all. Instead they are small, gray, land-dwelling crustaceans called isopods that are related to shrimp and crayfish. They have hard, shell-like coverings made up of several plates, three body sections, seven pairs of legs, and two antennae.

Sowbug

While sowbugs and pillbugs are very similar looking, pillbugs can roll up into a ball when disturbed, which is why they are sometimes called "roly-polies." Both are active at night and feed on dead and decaying plant material. During the day, they can be found under leaf litter, logs, or rocks.

Pillbug

Snails and **Slugs** are slow-moving, slimy invertebrates called gastropods. They are commonly found in yards and gardens. Both have a fleshy, typically brown or gray unsegmented body without legs, and two pairs of retractable tentacles off the head. The upper two tentacles have eyes. Both snails and slugs secrete mucus or "slime" to help them move and prevent them from drying out. Snails, but not slugs, also have a hard shell for protection.

Snail

Slug

Activity: Insect—or Not?

Circle the pictures below that show insects.

1. Spider

2. Wasp

3. Centipede

4. Earthworm

5. Carpenter Ant

6. Pillbug

7. Butterfly

8. Leafhopper

9. Millipede

10. Scorpion

11. Beetle

12. Grasshopper

Answers on page 105! ☞

Get to Know the Major Groups of Insects

There are more than 20 major groups (orders) of insects, but the most-common and familiar insects belong to a few major groups. By getting to know them, you can learn to identify many of the insects you'll see around.

Insects			
Coleoptera Beetles		**Hemiptera** True Bugs	
Lepidoptera Butterflies and Moths		**Blattodea** Cockroaches and Termites	
Odonata Dragonflies and Damselflies		**Mantodea** Praying Mantises	
Hymenoptera Bees, Wasps, and Ants		**Phasmida** Walking Sticks	
Orthoptera Grasshoppers, Crickets, and Katydids		**Ephemeroptera** Mayflies	
Diptera Flies		**Dermaptera** Earwigs	

Beetles belong to the order Coleoptera. They represent about 40% of all known insects and have more species than any other group of animals on Earth. Adult beetles tend to be rather large, clumsy insects. Most have a hard exoskeleton, almost like a suit of armor, and strong legs that end in a noticeable paired claw. Beetles also have two pairs of wings, but they aren't always easy to see. The first pair is modified into protective covers, called **elytra**. When closed, they conceal the larger wings underneath. This unique feature separates them from most other insects. Beetles also have two prominent antennae, but their exact shape varies a lot between species. All beetles have chewing mouthparts called mandibles, which are hard and almost tooth-like.

Quick ID Tips:

- Oval to somewhat elongated body
- Hard exoskeleton
- Four (4) pairs of wings
- First pair of wings is hardened (elytra)
- Chewing mouthparts (mandibles)
- Two (2) antennae that vary in shape

Colorado Potato Beetle

Six-spotted Tiger Beetle

Eastern Firefly

Lady Beetle

Get to Know the Major Groups of Insects

Butterflies and **Moths** belong to the order Lepidoptera. This is the second-largest group of insects and includes some of the largest and most beautiful creatures. Butterflies and moths have two pairs of obvious, often large, transparent wings. The wings are partially or completely covered by many tiny scales that give them their color and pattern. Most butterflies and moths have elongated, relatively skinny bodies; two large compound eyes; and tube-like mouthparts called a **proboscis** for sipping fluid. They also have two antennae that vary somewhat in shape but are often long and thin or ferny-looking.

Fast Fact: Bats love to eat moths, and they hone in on them using ultrasound (sound too high for human ears to hear). But many moth species can hear ultrasound, too, and they react to the sound of an approaching bat!

Quick ID Tips:

- Often large and colorful or with elaborate patterns
- Four (4) wings
- Wings covered in many tiny scales
- Two (2) large compound eyes
- Long, often slender bodies
- Tube-like mouthparts (proboscis)
- Antennae are long and thin with a nob at the end (butterflies) or ferny-looking (moths)

Cecropia Moth

Tersa Sphinx Moth

Mourning Cloak Butterfly

Giant Swallowtail Butterfly

Dragonflies and **Damselflies** belong to the insect order Odonata. They are a relatively small group of insects, but easy to spot. Good fliers, adults have two pairs of transparent membranous wings, each with many small veins, and some have colorfully patterned wings. Dragonflies and damselflies have long, slender bodies; a noticeable rounded head with large compound eyes; and chewing mandibles. Dragonflies are generally larger than damselflies, fly fast, and hold their wings outstretched when at rest. Damselflies are generally smaller and more delicate-looking, have a slower, weaker flight, and fold their wings over their backs when resting.

Quick ID Tips:

- Large head
- Chewing mouthparts (mandibles)
- Two (2) large compound eyes
- Long, slender abdomen
- Two (2) short antennae
- Four (4) transparent wings

Fast Fact: Dragonflies today can reach impressive sizes, but nothing compared to hundreds millions of years ago, when some dragonflies reached more than a foot in wingspan. They could grow so big because there was more oxygen available in the atmosphere.

Damselfly perching

Dragonfly perching

Meadowhawk Dragonfly

Twelve-spotted Skimmer Dragonfly

Tule Bluet Damselfly

Sedge Sprite Damselfly

Get to Know the Major Groups of Insects

Bees, Wasps, Ants, and **Sawflies** belong to the insect order Hymenoptera. Adults tend to be relatively small in size. They have two pairs of transparent wings (although some individuals may lack wings) and have two fairly large compound eyes and two antennae that tend to be thin but not very long. Most have chewing mouthparts and bodies with a noticeably narrow waist between the abdomen and thorax. The females of many species have a stinger on the abdomen. Many, but not all, species are social and live in nests or large colonies.

Fast Fact: While you might think that all bees and wasps live together in a hive, that's not true. Many native bees are solitary nesters and live alone. They often nest in the ground, in soil, or wood.

Quick ID Tips:

- Four (4) transparent wings
- Two (2) large compound eyes
- Narrow waist (petiole)
- Mostly chewing mouthparts
- Stinger on tip of abdomen in females
- Ants have elbowed antennae

Common Eastern Bumblebee

Eastern Yellowjacket

Giant Ichneumonid Wasp

Carpenter Ant

Flies belong to the insect order Diptera. Adults tend to be small, with somewhat compact hairy bodies. They only have one pair of visible transparent wings. (This is important for telling them apart from bees and wasps.) The rear wings are reduced to small, club-like structures called halteres. They help stabilize the insect when it is flying. Flies have two large compound eyes, very short antennae, and a variety of different mouthparts designed for piercing, lapping, or sponging up liquids.

Quick ID Tips:

- Oval, hairy body
- Two transparent wings
- Rear wings reduced to club-like structures (halters)
- Two large compound eyes
- Two (2) short antennae
- Piercing and sucking mouthparts

23

Fast Fact: Flies might get a bad reputation because of the house fly or the mosquito, but many flies are important pollinators, act as nature's "garbage crew," or get squished after being mistaken for huge "mosquitoes" like the crane fly shown below. (But crane flies don't bite; in fact, they can't! Their mouthparts are only good for sopping up liquids.)

Halteres on a Crane Fly

House Fly

Green Bottle Fly

Common Hover Fly

Robber Fly

Crane Fly

Get to Know the Major Groups of Insects

Grasshoppers, Crickets, and **Katydids** belong to the insect order Orthoptera. Adults tend to be relatively large insects with elongated, thick bodies and two pairs of wings. The first pair is narrow and somewhat thickened. They cover a second larger, wider pair underneath. Both pairs of wings are held over the back when at rest. The hind legs are long and powerful and used for jumping. They have relatively large compound eyes, chewing mouthparts, and thin antennae that may be long or short depending on the species.

Quick ID Tips:

- Cylindrical body shape
- Four (4) wings
- First pair of wings is thickened (membranous)
- Chewing mouthparts (mandibles)
- Long hind legs
- Two (2) large compound eyes
- Two (2) thin antennae that may be long or short
- Many produce sound (stridulation) by rubbing specialized organs on their wings or legs together

Fast Fact: Have you ever heard of a plague of locusts? Sometimes, populations of grasshoppers and locusts can explode, and the hungry insects then search for food. This happened on several occasions in the U.S. Midwest in the nineteenth century. These "grasshopper plagues" devastated crops, and there were sometimes so many insects that the skies went dark, with possibly trillions of insects in some swarms. Oddly, the main insect responsible is now extinct.

Lubber Grasshopper

Carolina Grasshopper

Fork-tailed Bush Katydid

Fall Field Cricket

Activity: Bee, Wasp, or Ant Challenge

Identify each bug below as either a bee, wasp, or ant.

1. _____

2. _____

3. _____

4. _____

5. _____

6. _____

7. _____

8. _____

9. _____

Answers on page 105! ☞

Get to Know the Major Groups of Insects

Cockroaches and **Termites** belong to the insect order Blattodea. Cockroaches are probably the most familiar insects in this group. Adults are generally brown in color and have oval and somewhat flattened bodies; very long, thin antennae; and two pairs of membranous wings. They are not good fliers and tend to crawl instead, often moving quickly when disturbed. They are active at night (nocturnal) and can often be found in homes or garages.

Fast Fact: Many insects are relatively short-lived (some mayflies live for a day or two), but adult cockroaches can live up to several years in ideal circumstances.

Quick ID Tips:

- Oval, flattened body
- Two (2) long, thin antennae
- Four (4) membranous wings
- Chewing mouthparts

Walking Sticks belong to the insect order Phasmida. They have chewing mouthparts and very long legs, bodies, and antennae that help them look almost exactly like a small branch or a stick.

Fast Fact: Most walking stick insects in North America are around 2–4 inches long, but some species found in Asia can be almost 2 feet long!

Quick ID Tips:

- Long, narrow body
- Six (6) long, thin legs
- Two (2) long, thin antennae
- Chewing mouthparts

American Cockroach

Termites

Northern Walking Stick

True Bugs belong to the insect order Hemiptera. Adults have a wide variety of body shapes but are often somewhat flattened and oval in appearance. They have two pairs of membranous wings. The front pair is often thickened at the base. True bugs hold their wings over their back when at rest, often forming an "X-shaped" pattern. They have fairly large compound eyes; slender beak-like mouthparts for piercing and sucking; and thin, often fairly long antennae.

Quick ID Tips:

- Flattened, oval body
- Four (4) membranous wings
- Front (4) wings thickened at the base
- Two (2) thin antennae
- Two (2) large compound eyes
- Slender beak-like mouthparts

Fast Fact: Technically speaking, not all insects are bugs. The order Hempitera consists of "true bugs" and examples include cicadas, leafhoppers, and aphids. But the term bug, as a general term, is often used to describe all insects, and even non-insects such as spiders, or other creepy-crawlies.

Red-banded Leafhopper

Milkweed Assassin Bug

Shield Bug

Woolly Aphid

Dog-day Cicada

Get to Know the Major Groups of Insects

Mayflies belong to the insect order Ephemeroptera. Adults have elongated, delicate-looking bodies; two pairs of transparent wings; short antennae; and three thin hair-like tails called filaments off the tip of their abdomen. They lack functional mouthparts and do not feed as adults.

Quick ID Tips:

- Elongated body
- Four (4) transparent wings
- Two (2) short antennae
- Three (3) long filaments off tip of abdomen
- No mouth

Fast Fact: Mayflies are often a good indicator of water quality, and when they emerge as adults, they often do so in huge numbers, enough to stop traffic or appear on weather radar as "clouds."

Earwigs belong to the insect order Dermaptera. They have elongated, flattened bodies with chewing mouthparts, thin antennae, and two pincer-like features called cerci off the tip of their abdomen. They are often found under logs, rocks, leaf litter, or even in flowerpots and they may occasionally wander into houses.

Quick ID Tips:

- Elongated, flattened body
- Chewing mouthparts
- Two (2) pincers off the tip of the abdomen (cerci)

Fast Fact: Earwigs have a bad reputation because of superstitions suggesting they crawl into human ears. They don't; what's more, they are actually harmless. The impressive looking pincers on the males are harmless and used to capture prey and defend themselves against other bugs.

Mayfly

European Earwig

Praying Mantises belong to the insect order Mantodea. These are large and bizarre-looking insects. Adults have long bodies, a unique triangular head with two large compound eyes, chewing mouthparts, and two pairs of wings. The front pair is narrow and thick. They are folded over the insect's back when at rest. Praying mantises also have long legs. The front pair is particularly large and powerful looking, has spines, and is adapted for capturing prey. They are often held upright in front of the insect when not used for walking.

Quick ID Tips:

- Long, narrow body
- Triangular head
- Two (2) large compound eyes
- Two (2) short antennae
- Four (4) membranous wings
- Six (6) long legs
- Front legs enlarged and with spines for holding prey
- Chewing mouthparts

Carolina Praying Mantis

Fast Fact: Carolina Praying Mantis females are larger than the males, and after mating, the female will sometimes eat the male. While gross, the added nutrients give her future offspring a better chance to survive.

Insect Life Cycle

All insects go through several different stages as they grow. This change is called **metamorphosis**. Insects have two different forms of metamorphosis.

Complete Metamorphosis

Most insects go through a **complete metamorphosis,** which consists of four different stages: **egg, larva, pupa,** and **adult**. Each stage looks very different from the others. The egg is the first stage of an insect's life cycle. Each egg is laid by a female insect. The egg hatches into a worm-like larva. The larva is the main feeding and growing stage. When done feeding, the larva turns into a pupa. The pupa is the transitional stage between the larva and adult. The final stage of an insect's life cycle is the adult. It emerges from a pupa and is the reproductive stage.

Insects that go through a complete metamorphosis include butterflies, moths, flies, beetles, bees, wasps, and ants.

Adult

Egg

Monarch Butterfly

Larva
(known as a caterpillar)

Pupa
(known as a chrysalis)

Insect Life Cycle

Incomplete Metamorphosis

Other insects go through **incomplete metamorphosis**. It has three stages: **egg, nymph,** and **adult**. In this type of metamorphosis, the nymphs look like smaller versions of the adults, except they lack wings and cannot reproduce.

Grasshoppers, walking sticks, praying mantises, dragonflies, damselflies, true bugs, earwigs, and cockroaches are examples of insects that go through an incomplete metamorphosis.

Quiz Time

1. Which of these insects goes through complete metamorphosis?

A. Grasshopper B. Dragonfly
C. House Fly D. Earwig

2. Sometimes, the nymphs that undergo incomplete metamorphosis live really different lives than the adult insects. Where do you think you'll find the nymphs of dragonflies?

A. In trees B. Underground
C. Flying around in the air
D. In water

Adult

Egg

Boxelder Bug

Nymph

Answers on page 105! ☞

Actual Size

Insects come in many different sizes. Some are small and can be easy to miss unless you look closely. Still others can be quite large and are very obvious.

Here are several common insects shown at their actual size:

Giant Swallowtail Butterfly Wingspan of 5.5 inches

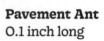

Green Aphid
0.125 inch long

Pavement Ant
0.1 inch long

Earwig
0.6 inch long

Red-legged Grasshopper
1 inch long

Northern Walking Stick 3.5 inches long

Green Stink Bug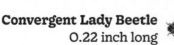
0.5 inch long

Convergent Lady Beetle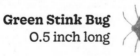
0.22 inch long

White-lined Sphinx Moth
Wingspan of 3.25 inches

Common Whitetail Dragonfly
Wingspan of 2.5 inches

American Cockroach
1.5 inches long

Orange Sulphur Butterfly
Wingspan of 2.25 inches

Quiz Time

Some insects in North America get big, like the Giant Swallowtail, which can reach nearly 6 inches in wingspan. The record for wingspan currently goes to the White Witch Moth, found in South America.

Just how big do you think its wingspan can get?

A. 8 inches
B. 9 inches
C. 10 inches
D. 11 inches

Large Milkweed Bug
0.6 inch long

June Beetle
0.6 inch long

Monarch Caterpillar
2 inches long

Polyphemus Moth Wingspan of 5.5 inches

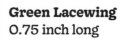

Greenbottle Fly
0.35 inch long

Green Lacewing
0.75 inch long

Mayfly
1 inch long

Answers on page 105! ☞

Insects Month-by-Month: The Northern US

Different insects may be active at different times of the year. Here is a general idea of when to look for certain species in the Northern US.

January	February	March	April	May	June
			Bumbleebees Common at flowers		
				Luna Moths One group of adults per year, attracted to artificial light	
				June Bugs Attracted to lights	
				Mayflies Adults found near water, attracted to light	
					Fireflies Adults active at dusk

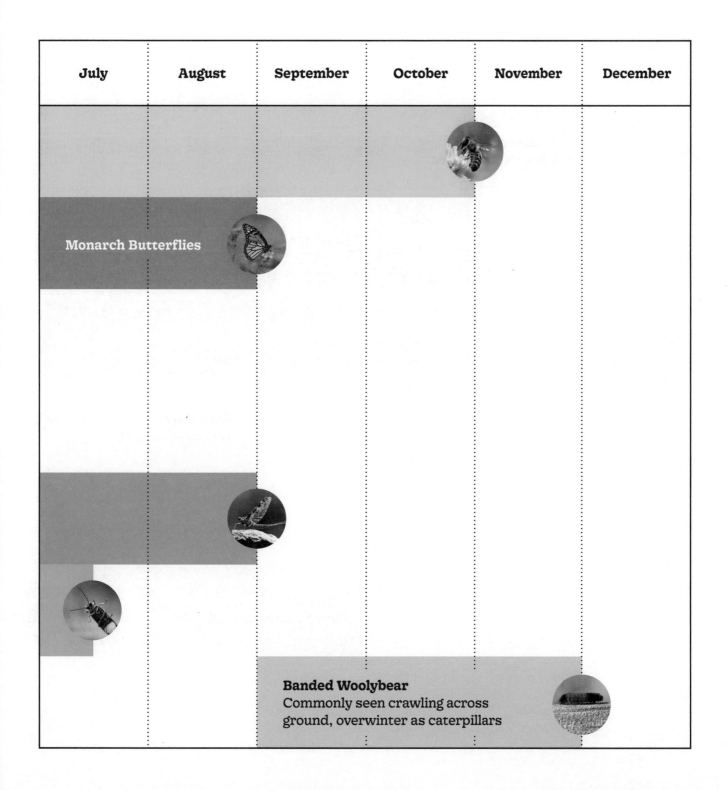

July	August	September	October	November	December

Monarch Butterflies

Banded Woolybear
Commonly seen crawling across
ground, overwinter as caterpillars

Insects Month-by-Month: The Southern US

Different insects may be active at different times of the year. Here is a general idea of when to look for certain species in the Southern US.

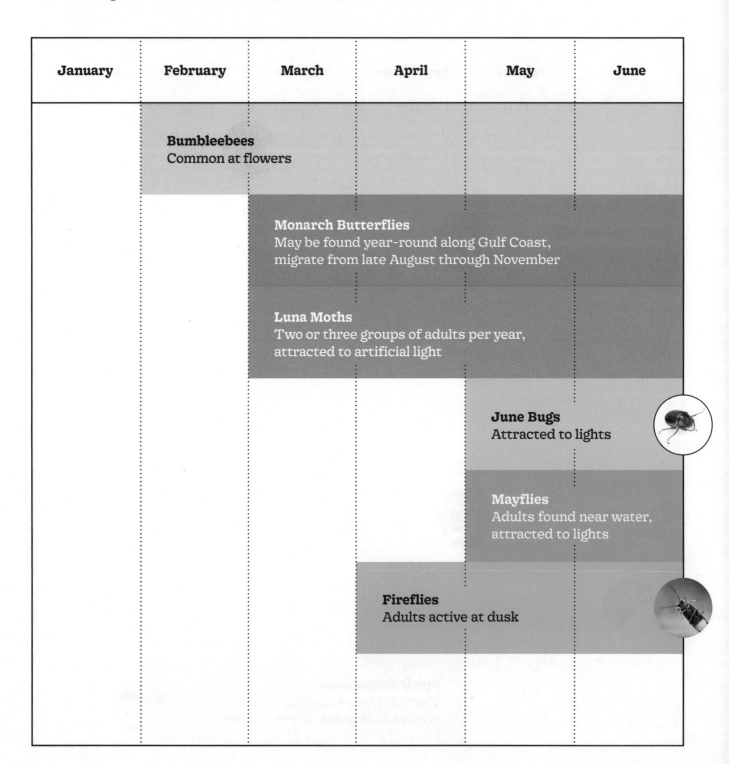

January	February	March	April	May	June

Bumbleebees
Common at flowers

Monarch Butterflies
May be found year-round along Gulf Coast, migrate from late August through November

Luna Moths
Two or three groups of adults per year, attracted to artificial light

June Bugs
Attracted to lights

Mayflies
Adults found near water, attracted to lights

Fireflies
Adults active at dusk

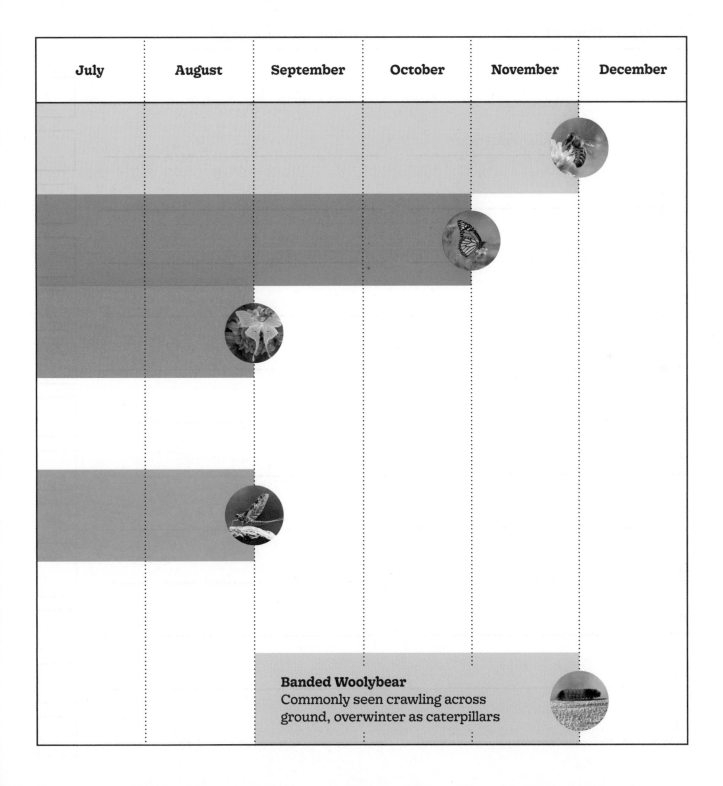

July	August	September	October	November	December

Banded Woolybear
Commonly seen crawling across
ground, overwinter as caterpillars

Activity: Insects I Want to See

Look through this book and your other favorite bug books to make a list of insects you want to see. Then, figure out the best time to look and where, and keep track of your finds here—check the box when you've seen it!

Insect I Want to See	**When & Where to Find It**	👍
Example: Monarch Butterfly	*Summer, on milkweed*	☐
1.		☐
2.		☐
3.		☐
4.		☐
5.		☐
6.		☐
7.		☐
8.		☐
9.		☐
10.		☐
11.		☐
12.		☐
13.		☐

Insect I Want to See   **When & Where to Find It**   👍

14. _____   _____   ☐

15. _____   _____   ☐

16. _____   _____   ☐

17. _____   _____   ☐

18. _____   _____   ☐

19. _____   _____   ☐

20. _____   _____   ☐

21. _____   _____   ☐

22. _____   _____   ☐

23. _____   _____   ☐

24. _____   _____   ☐

25. _____   _____   ☐

26. _____   _____   ☐

27. _____   _____   ☐

28. _____   _____   ☐

29. _____   _____   ☐

30. _____   _____   ☐

Insect I Want to See   **When & Where to Find It**

Native and Non-native vs. Invasive

A **native** organism is a species that occurs naturally within a particular area or region. A **non-native** organism is one that occurs outside of its natural range. It may have arrived in the new area by accident (like the emerald ash borer), or have been brought there on purpose by people (like honeybees). Some non-native species are also considered invasive. An **invasive** species causes harm to its new environment, other species that naturally occur there, or to the economy. But keep in mind that not all non-native species are invasive. Some, like the western honey bee have been very beneficial for pollinating crops (agriculture) and for honey production.

Invasive Insect Species

Red Imported Fire Ants are native to South America. Found throughout much of the southern United States, they have a painful sting and can cause damage to buildings, crops, other native wildlife, and the environment.

Multicolored Asian Lady Beetles are common throughout the United States but native to Asia. They hibernate over the winter in large groups and often invade homes and other buildings. They may also harm native lady beetles. Worse yet, they can bite!

Cabbage White Butterflies are common in gardens, roadsides, and farmers' fields. Native to Europe, they are one of the world's most widespread and abundant pest butterflies and feed on many vegetables.

Japanese Beetles are native to Japan. A common garden and lawn pest, they feed on over 300 different species of plants. They are found in many parts of the United States.

Mediterranean Fruit Flies are native to Africa. Considered one of the most destructive fruit pests in the world, they have been found in Florida, California, Texas, and Hawaii.

Gypsy Moths are a common forest pest in the Northeast and parts of the Midwest, and they can cause complete tree defoliation (they eat all the leaves) and can even kill trees. They are native to Europe.

Non-native (but not Invasive) Insect Species

Western Honeybees are common in the United States and Canada. They are native to Europe, the Middle East, and Africa.

European Skippers, common across the northern United States and southern Canada, aren't considered pests and are native to Europe.

Activity: Native or Non-native?

A huge number of plants, animals, and insects have been introduced (accidentally or on purpose) to North America since settlers and colonizers first arrived. Insects are no exception. Some are so familiar and widespread it might be surprising that they actually originated somewhere else. Others are more-recent introductions and are invasive, outcompeting native insects and causing a great deal of damage to the environment.

The following insects are all relatively familiar or have been in the news lately. Can you guess which ones are native and non-native? Label each picture on the right with native or non-native. Bonus points if you can recognize (circle) the invasive ones!

This beautiful beetle is the non-native (and invasive) Emerald Ash Borer, which has done tremendous damage to ash trees in many parts of the United States.

1. Flame Skipper

_____

2. Cabbage White Butterfly

_____

3. European Skipper

_____

4. Brown Marmorated Stink Bug

_____

5. Gypsy Moth

_____

6. European Spruce Bark Beetle

_____

7. Emerald Ash Borer

_____

8. Giant Leopard Moth

_____

9. Eyed Elater

_____

10. Asian Tiger Mosquito

_____

Native   **Non-native**   **Invasive**

Answers on page 105! ☞

Examine Habitats, Make a Hypothesis, Then Go Look

Go outside in your yard, a nearby park, or even the schoolyard and pick an area with some vegetation. For instance, a spot with several different types of blooming flowers (even weeds!) or leafy plants is a great place to start. Now, look closely at the plants and surrounding environment. What do you see? Do you notice any insects? If so, how many do you see, where are they, and what are they doing? Do you observe any differences between the various flowers or plants the insects are on? Think about things such as flower color, leaf size or shape, plant height, or any other unique characteristics.

Now, imagine that you observed more insects on the flowers of one plant (let's call it plant 1) than compared to a different type (plant 2). Next, ask a question or two based on the observations you made. For example, "Why are so many more insects visiting the flowers of plant 1 compared to plant 2?" Finally, develop a hypothesis or two that provides a possible answer to each question you have. *A hypothesis is a suggested explanation for an observation or phenomenon. It can be tested by making observations.*

So, a possible hypothesis might be: More insects visited plant 1 because it has a higher abundance of flowers that provide food in the form of pollen and nectar than plant 2. (This, of course, is just one of many possible explanations.)

The last step is to think about how you could test your hypothesis. What different types of information or data would you need to collect and how would you collect it?

For this hypothesis, counting and comparing the total number of individual flowers on both plants would be a good start. This would give you valuable data that could be used to support or reject the hypothesis. Better yet, paying attention in this way, and making predictions (and seeing if they are correct or not), will help you learn to identify plants and where you're likely to find certain types of insects in the future. (For example, if you want to see monarch butterflies or caterpillars, you'll want to learn to identify milkweed, where monarch adults lay eggs and larvae chomp away at the leaves.)

Activity: Compare and Contrast

Now you try: Find two or more flowering plants to compare. Start out by picking one plant where you already see bugs. Compare that one to a flowering plant that has fewer visitors. Watch each one for the same amount of time (5 minutes, say), and count how many insects visit it or are nearby it. Then, describe both, and then make a hypothesis about why one plant had more bugs than the other.

Plant 1

Plant Height/Description:

_____

_____

Flowers?

_____

Flower Description:

_____

_____

How many bugs?

_____

What were they doing?

_____

_____

My Hypothesis

_____

_____

_____

_____

Plant 2

Plant Height/Description:

_____

_____

Flowers?

_____

Flower Description:

_____

_____

How many bugs?

_____

What were they doing?

_____

_____

Fast Fact

Sometimes "weeds," such as dandelions or clovers, offer more resources to insects than some garden plants (say, hostas, for example).

Explore Various Habitats

Insects can be found in almost any habitat. However, most are very small and like to hide. As a result, many can be easily overlooked unless you know how and where to look.

The following list of insect habitats are easy to find and are home to a wide range of different insects and other arthropods:

1. Under logs or rocks
2. On flowers
3. Near dead wood
4. On leaves
5. In or near water
6. In or near buildings

Think about each of these habitats. How are they similar and different? Then make a hypothesis about the types of insects you might find in each.

My Hypothesis: I think I'll find these insects in the following environments:

1. Under logs or rocks:

_____

_____

2. On flowers:

_____

_____

3. Near dead wood:

_____

_____

4. On leaves:

_____

_____

5. In or near water:

_____

_____

6. In or near buildings:

_____

_____

Painted Lady Butterfly on Purple Coneflower

Habitat: Logs or Rocks

When you spot a log or rock on the ground, it might not look at first like a great place to find insects. However, the damp, dark spaces underneath provide great habitat or shelter for a wide range of different insects and other arthropods. All you need to do is explore.

This beetle was found hiding beneath a rock.

Before starting, though, it might be useful to have a few handy supplies. These include:

1. A clear plastic jar with a lid (old peanut butter jars are perfect)
2. A magnifying glass to examine what you find
3. A pair of tweezers or a small stick to move small objects or organisms
4. Gloves to protect your hands

Now, with your supplies handy, it's time to go outside. Once you find a log or larger rock, take a few minutes and just look at the area around it. Next, carefully roll the log or rock over. Be prepared to look quickly, as many organisms will run away when disturbed. Use the plastic jar to temporarily capture any critters for closer examination. Next, closely inspect the underside of the log or rock and the ground beneath. Use the magnifying glass to study some of the smaller organisms or use the tweezers to remove small leaves, bark, or other debris to see what lies underneath.

Once you are done exploring, always gently roll the log or rock back over to its original position Remember, the log or rock provides a home to many different creatures. Then you can move on to the next adventure.

Some of the common insects and arthropods that you might find under logs or rocks include:

Earwigs and eggs

Beetles

Ants

Cockroaches

Earthworms

Centipedes

Sow and Pill Bugs

Spiders

Habitat: Flowers

Flowers are another great place to find insects. They offer insects food in the form of pollen and nectar and attract a wide range of different species. This abundance of activity also attracts predators that seek to capture and eat unsuspecting flower visitors. (So if you look closely, you may find spiders or ambush bugs waiting for lunch or dinner.)

Flowers are also very common. They could be flowers in your garden, in a container on a patio, or even flowers (or weeds) in a nearby field or park. Once you locate some, don't immediately examine them up close. Stand back a few feet and see what you observe. Why type of insects might you expect to see? If the flowers are brightly colored and attractive, you should see a fair amount of activity, particularly from larger insects.

Next, look more closely. Examine a few flowers and you may see a variety of smaller, less obvious insects and arthropods directly on or in the flower. A magnifying glass can help spot them. Many of the insects visiting flowers are considered pollinators.

Take notice of what the various organisms are doing. Are they flying from one flower to another, sitting on the flower, or crawling inside the flower itself? These different behaviors vary widely between different insect species and groups, and they can tell you about the insect or critter, what it eats, and its lifecycle.

As you continue to watch, you will quickly discover that different flowers attract different insects, and that some types, colors, and sizes are much more attractive than others.

American Hover Fly

Note: Not all flower-visiting insects are active during the daytime. To see other cool species, try looking around sunset.

As an example, you may spot various hawk moths. They have long tongues (proboscises) and feed at flowers like hummingbirds.

Hummingbird Clearwing Moth

Some of the common insects that you might find on flowers include:

Bees

Butterflies

Flies

Beetles

Wasps

Day-flying Moths

Some of the common predators that you might find on flowers include:

Spiders

Ambush Bugs

Praying Mantises

Robber Flies

Habitat: Water

Many insects live in or near water for a portion of their life cycles. Streams, creeks, ponds, and lakes are often great places to look. However, be very careful around any body of water. Rocks, branches, logs, and muddy banks can be slippery and dangerous. Always have a parent or adult with you, and wear a life jacket for safety when exploring these habitats. Before starting, though, it might be useful to have a few handy supplies.

1. A large clear plastic jar with lid
2. A small aquarium net
3. Binoculars

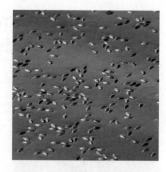

Swarming Whirligig Beetles

Approach the water slowly and watch for activity around the edges of the water and nearby vegetation. Think about what types of insects you might expect to find near the edge, on the water's surface, and in the water. Many insects spend at least part of their life cycle in the water; examples include mosquitoes, dragonflies, and more. And adult insects also spend a lot of time near water, flying around the area or perching on fallen branches, rocks, twigs, or other vegetation at the water's edge. Now, slowly scan the surface of the water. Pay attention to any movement or ripples. What do you see? Last, look below the surface of the water if it's clear. In shallow spots, you can use the aquarium net to gently dredge the bottom. Empty the net contents into a clear plastic jar and partially fill it with water. Wait a few minutes for any sediment to settle and then look closely.

What can you see? Once you are finished observing, remember to always release the organisms back into the water where you collected them.

Note: If you can't find a pond, stream, or creek, try looking in a birdbath or any container that has been full of rainwater for some time. You are likely to find mosquito larvae and maybe a few other small critters.

Some of the common insects that you might find near or on the surface of the water include:

Water Striders

Whirligig Beetles

Backswimmers

Some of the common insects that you might find in the water include:

Diving Beetles

Dragonfly and Damselfly Nymphs

Water Boatmen

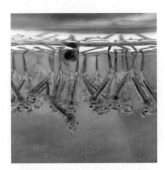

Mosquito Larvae

Giant Water Bugs

Habitat: Dead Wood

Dead trees, tree stumps, and fallen logs provide great habitat for many insects and other arthropods. Many live under the loose bark. Others live in the dead or decaying wood itself. Be very careful around dead trees and larger stumps. Some can be unstable or have branches or larger pieces that can fall.

Before starting, it might be useful to have a few handy supplies:

1. A clear plastic jar with a lid (an old peanut butter jar, for example)
2. A magnifying glass to examine what you find
3. A pair of forceps or a small sturdy stick to help remove bark or move small objects or organisms
4. Gloves

Once you locate a safe dead tree, stump, or fallen log, start by carefully looking over the outside. Think about what insects and other arthropods you might expect to find. Do you spot any organisms? Are there any small holes, webs, or sawdust that indicate activity?

Next, look for any loose bark. The dark, cool spaces under bark provide shelter and other resources for many insects. Take the forceps or the sturdy stick and carefully remove pieces of the loose bark to see what lives underneath. Look quickly, as many critters will rapidly scatter when disturbed. Use the clear plastic jar to temporarily capture any creatures of interest for closer inspection. Remember to also look at the underside of the bark that you removed.

Once the bark is removed, look at the dead or decaying wood underneath more carefully. Use your magnifying glass to examine the wood surface in greater detail. Do you see any small holes, tunnels, or sawdust? Such signs may indicate current organism activity or a history of past activity, such as by wood-boring insects or insect

Fallen trees provide great habitat for many insects and other arthropods

nests. If the wood is decayed enough, you can also gently remove small portions of it to see what insects might be living inside.

Some of the common arthropods, insects, or signs of insects that you might find under bark or in decaying or dead wood include:

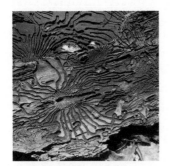

Bark Beetle Galleries (tunnels)

Carpenter Bee (or other native bee) Nest

Wood Wasp (also called Horntails)

Ants and their brood

Termites

Centipedes

Spiders and Daddy Longlegs

Earwigs

The time of year also may affect what you find. For example, carpenter bees nest in wood. In spring, they begin to excavate tunnels, creating perfectly round holes in which they will lay their eggs. Coarse sawdust below a hole is a sign of activity. By contrast, many insects and other arthropods overwinter under bark or in cavities in wood. Such locations are safe and secure sites to survive the cold winter months. Some insects, like lady beetles or boxelder bugs, even gather in large numbers. So, don't just limit your exploration to the summer months!

Boxelder Bugs

Habitat: Buildings

Some insects can even be found in buildings. Most occasionally wander into homes, garages, or basements looking for food or shelter. Most tend to be seen in cool, dark, and damp areas or at night when the lights are out. So even on a rainy day outside, you can go on a bug hunt inside. Some good places to check include around drains or showers; near doors or on windowsills; under objects such as interior door mats; in cool, moist areas of a basement; or near sources of food.

Some supplies you may want to have before you go explore include:

1. A large clear plastic jar with lid
2. A magnifying glass
3. A flashlight

Some of the common insects or anthropods that you might find in buildings include:

Jumping Spiders

House Flies

Earwigs

Silverfish

Cockroaches

Millipedes

Centipedes

Next, check around the outside of your home or school building. Looks for signs of activity such as spider webs, cocoons, or nests. Some great places to check include any building corners, where the roof of a building meets the wall, or along driveway or sidewalk cracks.

Some of the common insects or anthropods that you might find near buildings include:

Ant Nests

Paper Wasp Nests

Orb-weaving Spiders

Moth Caterpillars

Lastly, check around any outdoor lights after dark. Porch, garage, or security lights all attract a wide range of nocturnal (active at night) insects. Wait until just after dark. Then, go outside and find a light. Warm and cloudy summer nights are typically best. Watch the area immediately around the light as you approach. You might see a number of insects whirling around the light itself.

Habitat: Buildings

Next, check the walls, ceilings, and even the ground around the light. Many insects often land and hang out in these areas. Look closely and see how many different insects you can find. More insects will likely be attracted throughout the late evening and night, so you may want to check periodically. You may often see very different insects at different times. If you spot something cool, use the jar to temporarily capture it and take a closer look. You may even find a few predators that show up to take advantage of the abundant food.

Always be careful when going outside at night and let a parent or other adult know where you are going.

Some of the common insects or anthropods that you might find at a light at night include:

Moths   Beetles (including June Bugs)   Mayflies   Craneflies

Green Lacewings   Antlions   Praying Mantises

Habitat: Plants

Plants provide insects with many resources, including food, shelter, and nesting sites. Well over half of all insect species feed on plants (such animals are called **herbivores**). They may feed on, or in, almost every part of a plant, from stems, sap, and leaves to roots, flower bugs, and fruit. That means that it's often quite easy to find insects and other arthropods on plants, if you know how to look.

Monarch Butterfly

Before exploring, though, it may be handy to have the following supplies:

1. A clear plastic jar with lid for temporarily capturing any critters
2. A magnifying glass

Now, it's time to head outside and find some plants. Virtually any type or size of plant will do, whether it's the branches of a large tree to the blades of grass in a lawn. When you find a plant you want to check out, take few minutes to carefully inspect it. Looks for signs of feeding to start, such as chewed holes in leaves or along leaf edges, rolled leaves, or spotting or patterns on the leaves. If you find any signs of feeding, inspect these areas more closely. Be sure to look under the leaves and on other plant parts as well. Many plant-feeding insects are well camouflaged and can be hard to see unless you really look hard.

You can also put down a white sheet or cloth under a branch or around a plant and hit the plant with a stick. Be careful not to damage the plant though. This will knock off many critters on the sheet below where they can be more closely observed or temporarily captured using a clear jar.

Some of the common insects or arthropods that you might find on plants include:

Grasshoppers

Katydids

Caterpillars

Walking Sticks

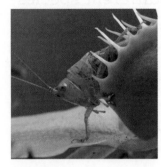

Praying Mantises

Spiders

Beetles

Project: Backyard Blitz

Now that you know how to look and what to look for, you can carry out a "Backyard Blitz." A take on "BioBlitz," it involves finding and identifying as many different species as possible in a specific area in a relatively short period of time. Such intensive surveys are often carried out by researchers in collaboration with a larger group of public volunteers, called community scientists. They work together to record a detailed list of the animal and plant life of a particular location.

You can do the same thing right in your own backyard or in a nearby park or field. It's a fun way to learn about the really cool and diverse insect life right outside your door.

Before you get started, though, here are a few things you will need:

1. A clear plastic jar with lid to temporarily capture any critters you find
2. A pencil and notebook to record and draw
3. A field guide to help you identify what you find

Now, head outside and start looking. Remember the different habitats discussed earlier, such as on several plants, under logs or stones, at flowers, and in or near water. Searching a variety of different habitats will help you find the maximum number of different insects and other arthropods. Keep track of your personal record number of insects and your "life list" for that area. It's really fun to see how many new critters you can find!

BioBlitz

It's fun to conduct bioblitzes at different times or in different seasons of the year. Make a hypothesis about when you think you'll find the most species, and then get out there and find out!

Insect Lookalikes

Some insects look very similar to one another. In many cases, this is on purpose. The close resemblance—called mimicry—provides a benefit to one or both organisms, such as protection from a predator. For example, many wasps can sting to defend themselves. The yellow-and-black pattern on the abdomen of wasps is an example of an **aposematic** or "warning" coloration. It serves to warn predators about the painful sting and instructs them to avoid such insects to stay safe. Not all insects can sting, of course; some insects have chemicals in their body (this is called chemical defense) that make them taste really bad if eaten.

Some insects have adapted to have a "warning" color pattern even though they aren't actually protected by the ability to sting or chemicals that given them a bad taste. They do this to fool predators into staying away. Other insects mimic a color pattern to help reinforce the overall message to predators: stay away.

From top to bottom, left to right: Hover Fly, Eastern Bumblebee, Northern Paper Wasp, and Bee-like Robber Fly.

Activity: Which Insects Can Sting?

Circle the following insects below that can sting.

1. Bumblebee

2. Honeybee

3. Bee Fly

4. Hummingbird
Clearwing Moth

5. Hover Fly

6. Yellowjacket

7. Locust Borer Beetle

8. Robber Fly

Answers on page 105! ☞

Activity: Which Insects Taste Bad?

Circle the following insects below that you think taste bad to predators.

1. Pipevine Swallowtail Butterfly

2. Monarch Butterfly

3. Viceroy Butterfly

4. Eastern Black Swallowtail

5. Spicebush Swallowtail Butterfly

Answers on page 105! ☞

Find a Dead Bug? Make It Part of Your Collection

Building a collection is a great way to learn about insects. Scientists use collections to study life on Earth, and to track changes of individual species, their populations, and the communities in which they live over time. Collections help us understand the past and present and enable us to better predict the future.

It is fun and easy to start a collection of your own. Before getting started, though, here is a list of some useful supplies:

1. An insect display case or storage box with foam bottom
2. Forceps or tweezers
3. Insect pins (sizes #2 and #3 are most useful; they are available online)
4. A few sheets of paper to make labels
5. A small plastic food storage container with lid
6. Paper towels

When exploring inside or out, you will likely find a dead insect or arthropod. This is a great way to start your collection, especially if you don't want to harm any bugs. First, use the forceps or your hand to gently pick up the specimen. Next, check to see if it is still flexible. Do this by seeing if its legs, body, or wings move at all with a light touch. If it is still flexible, you can directly add it to your collection.

Grab an insect pin and the insect storage box. Place the insect on the foam bottom of the box. Next, insert the pin as straight as you can through the insect's thorax from top to bottom and into the foam. Leave about ¼ inch of the pin sticking out the top of the insect. This will allow you to easily handle the specimen using only the top portion of the pin.

Pinned Tomato Hornworm Moth

If the insect you found is hard and rigid, it will need to be relaxed a bit before it can be safely pinned. If not, the specimen will break when pinned. To do this, you will need to create a small relaxing chamber. Place 2-4 sheets of wet paper towels flat in the bottom of the plastic food storage container. There should be no standing water. Next, place the insect on the paper towels and securely close the lid. The exact amount of relaxing time needed varies with the size of the insect, but typically 24 hours is enough. **Note:** Avoid leaving the specimen in the chamber for too long. This can result in mold growth or otherwise rot the specimen. When a specimen's legs, body, or wings are flexible, then it can be pinned.

Finally, all specimens should have a label. This is a small piece of paper that should be placed on the pin below each insect specimen. Labels provide important scientific information about the specimen, including:

Entomological Collection

1. The name of the collector (*Example: Molly Kim*)
2. The location it was collected (*Example: Caledonia, Wisconsin*)
3. The date of collection (*Example: May 23, 2019*)

Build a Bug House for a Pet Bug

Many bugs can make fun pets. But just like us, they need a good home to be happy. Building a bug house is fairly easy. Here are a few supplies that you'll need:

Praying Mantis

1. A small reptile terrarium with a mesh lid (available from most pet stores)
2. A small bag of sterile sand or potting soil
3. A medium-size rock
4. A few dead twigs
5. The lid to a jar
6. A cotton ball
7. A floral tube (used in bouquets to keep vegetation fresh; available at florist shops)

Place about 1 inch of sand or soil in the bottom of the terrarium. Place the rock on one side and add the branches. Arrange them so that they are supported by the sides of the terrarium and enable the insect to crawl upwards. Finally, place a wet cotton ball in the jar lid and place it on the ground inside the terrarium. This will provide a water source; don't provide a bowl of water or standing water for the insect, as bugs can drown relatively easily.

Keep a Pet Bug

Now it's time to add a bug or two. Several insects make particularly good pets. Here are some to consider and how many the terrarium on page 75 can hold of that species. (Don't fill your bug house with more than one type of the below insects, however.)

1. 3-5 Crickets (these can be purchased at a pet store)
2. 1-2 Katydids
3. 1-3 Grasshoppers (particularly the Eastern Lubber Grasshopper)
4. 1-2 Walking Sticks
5. 1 Praying Mantis

Walking Sticks make great pet bugs!

Crickets are probably one of the easiest insects to maintain. They will eat lettuce, apple slices, carrots, potato, and squash for starters. Many grasshoppers will feed on such foods as well. If you collect a critter from outside, simply note what the insect was feeding on when captured and continue to provide those same leaves in the cage. It's important, but easy, to keep vegetation fresh: a floral tube (the tubes at the bottom of flower bouquets) filled with water can be used to help keep cut vegetation fresh.

The most important things to remember are that these are living creatures, just like dogs or cats. They need clean conditions, good food, and daily care to be happy. This means that you should check on them each day and provide new food regularly as needed, typically every other day, and add a bit of water to the cotton ball. Many are also good escape artists, taking advantage of even the smallest gaps, so always securely attach the mesh lid to the top of the terrarium. If you take good care of your insect pets, they will provide many hours of enjoyment.

The Praying Mantis

The only exception to the instructions above on this list is the praying mantis. It is a predator and needs to eat living insects. Happily, this bug is not picky. Flies, bugs, small grasshoppers, crickets, and moths are often easy to catch.

Find and Raise a Caterpillar

Many butterfly and moth caterpillars are easy to find and can be fun to raise. Taking care of caterpillars takes time, but it gives you the opportunity to watch them grow and eventually turn into adult insects. Caterpillars have relatively simple needs. They require a regular supply of fresh plant material; clean conditions; and a safe, secure, and roomy house. There are a number of different containers you can use, depending on the size of the caterpillar. While plastic containers are useful, often a terrarium with a mesh lid or mesh pop-up cage are the best options. A 14- or 24-inch mesh pop-up cage is inexpensive and can be purchased online. It is lightweight, unbreakable, and provides good air circulation. A floral tube or plastic bottle with water is best used to hold plant material and keep it fresh.

In general, you should only rear caterpillars that you find on plants. This will ensure that you know the correct food for them. Once you locate a caterpillar, use a pair of clippers to carefully cut the off branch on which it is located. Make note of the plant. This is its preferred food, and you will need to feed the caterpillar fresh cuttings from this type of plant only.

Place the stems of the plant material into a plastic bottle filled with water. Make sure that the gap between the branches at the top of the bottle is not large; otherwise, the caterpillar could crawl down into the water and drown. Place the bottle with the leaves in the mesh cage and place the caterpillar on the leaves. Replace the leaves and clean out the droppings in the cage regularly. Remember that the caterpillar needs good food and a clean home to be happy and grow.

Vegetation prepared for caterpillars.

When the caterpillar is fully grown, it will often crawl off the leaves and wander. It is now looking or a place to pupate or spin a cocoon. Once it has done so, check the cage periodically. The adult butterflies and moths will often emerge in a few weeks. If it is late summer or early fall and the butterfly or moth has not emerged after about 4 weeks, it may overwinter and emerge in spring. Place the cage in a cool, dark location like a basement or garage until warm weather returns.

Monarch caterpillar

Once your butterfly or moth emerges, observe it for a bit. Use a field guide to see if you can identify what it is. Once you have, take the cage outside and let the moth or butterfly free in your yard or nearby park.

Hunt for Mosquito Larvae

Mosquitoes are flies that are commonly found in most outdoor areas. They are probably best known for producing painful and itchy bites. While adult mosquitos are terrestrial (live on land), their larvae are fully aquatic (live in water). They naturally occur in wetlands but can breed in almost any container with stagnant water, and this includes fountains, old tires, birdbaths, and plant saucers. Virtually any container that holds water is a possible habitat.

Now that you know a bit more about where to look, head outside and explore. Once you find a container with water, look closely just below the surface. Mosquito larvae are often called "wigglers" because of their frequent back-and forth thrashing movement, so pay attention to any movement or ripples. These wigglers eat almost anything they can find in the water.

Mosquito larvae have a long, thin brown body; no legs; and a round head. While they can swim, larvae spend most of their lives close to the water's surface, dangling with their head down and breathing through a long tube called a siphon off their tail. Even a small container can have a lot of them!

Once you find some, check on them each day. Mosquito larvae develop very quickly and soon form more chunky-looking pupae. They rest just below the surface of the water. Although the pupae do not feed, they can move, often flipping over like a somersault. Because of this behavior, they are often called "tumblers." The winged adults emerge in just a few days.

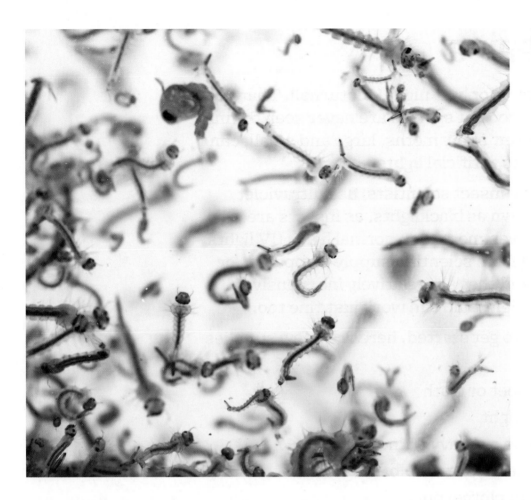

Once you've observed a few, look around in your yard for other places you might find mosquito larvae, and then dump out the water. (That way, you'll have fewer mosquitoes to bother you!)

Moth Trapping

Most moths are active only at night (nocturnal). That means many of the coolest species are never seen during the daytime. However, many moths, large and small, can be easily attracted to artificial lights.

Most entomologists (insect scientists) use ultraviolet lights (UV), also known as blacklights, as insects are attracted to them even more than normal light. UV lights are available online from scientific supply companies or elsewhere online, and they are relatively inexpensive. However, a regular light bulb can work just fine too.

When you're ready to get started, here are a few supplies that you'll need:

1. An old white sheet or cloth
2. A metal clamp light
3. A bundle of rope or heavy twine
4. A 100-watt incandescent bulb
5. 2 binder clips of clothespins
6. A long extension cord
7. 2 rocks

As this activity requires a little setup, its best to start well before sunset. You may also want to have a parent, adult, or sibling to help. First, locate two trees or posts. They should be about 5-7 feet apart. Tie one end of the rope to the first tree about 4-5 feet off the ground. Run the rope to the other tree, and loop the rope around the trunk at least once, making sure that the rope between the trees is level and taut. Next, run the rope up the tree trunk about 1 foot, loop it around once more, and run it over to the first tree. Tie it to the first tree again, making sure it is level and taut. Now, hang the white sheet on the lower rope, securing it to the rope with binder clips or clothespins. Pull the bottom of the sheet forward, creating a 90-degree angle with the ground and place a rock on both ends of the sheet to prevent it from blowing in the breeze. Remove the round metal shield from the clamp light, screw in a 100-

watt bulb, and clamp the light to the upper string so that it hangs downward. Attach it to an extension cord and plug the cord into an outlet. Finally, turn the light on.

You'll want to turn the light on about 30 minutes before dark. For best results, you'll want to choose a cloudy, dark night. Check the sheet periodically to see what moths and other insects arrive. You will be amazed!

Heading out with a flashlight in one hand and a camera in another is an easy way to record your finds (and identify them later).

Raspberry Pyrausta Moth at a light trap

Making Moth Bait

What You'll Need

- 1 can/bottle of stale beer (ask your parents)
- 1 can of fruit, preferably in heavy syrup, smashed up (can substitute overripe bananas)
- Several cups of brown sugar or molasses
- A large bowl
- A medium-size paintbrush
- A flashlight
- A camera (optional)

Not all moth species visit lights, but a good number of them will visit trees that are "painted" with moth bait. Moth bait is pretty simple to make, but you'll need an adult's help. You simply create a thick mixture of stale beer, crushed-up fruit, and enough brown sugar or molasses in a large bowl. It should be pretty sickly-sweet smelling by the time you are done. (That's how moths notice it: with their sense of smell).

Then, go out about 45 minutes before sunset and use a paintbrush to paint a 2x2-foot square onto a tree. Then repeat that on another tree or two, and wait until it gets dark.

Then, head out to the trees to see what moths (and other bugs) have shown up to feed! Often, you'll get to see moths unfurling their long straw-like **proboscis** to slurp up the sugary mix. Check back later throughout the night and see if other species show up!

Catch and Photograph Fireflies

Despite their name, fireflies or lightning bugs are actually beetles. They are particularly cool because they produce light. This process is called **bioluminescence**. Fireflies have a special light-producing organ at the tip of their abdomen called a "lantern." On summer evenings as the sun goes down, they fly slowly around and flash. Each species of firefly produces its own unique flash pattern. You can observe this amazing process close-up.

Firefly on a window

Before starting, here are just a few things you'll need:

1. A large clear plastic jar with lid
2. A smartphone with camera.

Okay, now you are ready. As the sun begins to go down, head outside and watch. You can explore your yard or a nearby field or park. In many areas, fireflies can be pretty common and numerous. They are most common in the eastern half of the country. Look for small flashes. You should see both moving flashes and stationary ones. The males are usually flying, while the females remain stationary. Follow the flashes until you spot a firefly. Use the large plastic jar to catch several insects.

Next, bring the jar inside and turn out the lights. Watch as the fireflies flash and pay particular attention to their lanterns. Now, use the smartphone, set the camera's video to slow motion, and take some video. When done, play the video back and watch. You can also do this outside to capture the activity from many different fireflies. Either way, it's amazing!

Cricket Math: Cricket Thermometers

Crickets are common insects. While you may not regularly see them, their chirping sound at night is loud and unmistakable. But did you know that crickets can actually tell the temperature? That's because they are **poikilotherms**, a large word for an organism that cannot internally regulate its body temperature. As a result, the muscles that control the movements of their wings and make the chirping sound contract faster or slower depending on the surrounding temperature. So, let's put it to a test.

Before we start, though, here are a few things that you'll need:

1. An outdoor thermometer
2. A stopwatch (you can also use a smartphone)
3. A pencil and paper

Now, place the thermometer outside at least 30 minutes ahead of time. As evening approaches, head outside and listen for chirping crickets. When you hear one, use the stopwatch to count the total number of chirps in 14 seconds and record that number on a sheet of paper. Next, add 40 to the number you recorded. Compare this number to the reading on the thermometer. They should be the same or very similar.

Equation: Total number of chirps in 14 seconds + 40 = the temperature.

Repeat this on cooler or warmer nights to see if you can hear the difference.

Cicada Cycle Math

Cicadas are strange creatures. While they look like large flies, cicadas are actually true bugs. Many different species of cicadas exist, but periodical cicadas are quite unique. They are probably best known for their very loud courtship calls and amazingly long life cycles. They are most famous for emerging in huge numbers periodically; these "broods" occur only every 13 or 17 years, depending on the exact species. The remaining portion of the time, cicadas are nymphs living and feeding underground and developing really, really slowly.

What is particularly unusual is that the 13- and 17-year cycles are actually prime numbers. A prime number is a number greater than one that is not a product of two smaller numbers. In other words, the number 13 can only be made by multiplying 1 by 13 and **not** by any other combination of numbers. The exact reason for this bizarre life cycle period is poorly understood by scientists.

Fast Fact

The cicada's very long life cycle makes it the longest-lived known insect!

Make a Bee Bundle Nest

Most native bees that you see are solitary. They do not live in large hives and are not aggressive. In fact, they are really beneficial to the environment, fun to watch, and easy to attract. Native bees do need a place to nest and you can help provide one!

One of the easiest bee nesting structures to make is a stem bundle. To get started, here are a few supplies that you will need:

1. A small bundle of reeds, bamboo, or hollow stems. Mixed sizes or materials are just fine.

2. Two large twist ties or zip ties

3. A 15-20-inch piece of wire

You can often find these right in your yard and cut them with a pair of clippers. Each piece should be about 6-8 inches long. Cut one end below a node (the slightly enlarged or ridged sections where the leaves attach) and the other above a node. This will ensure that one side is open (hollow) and the other end is closed. Cut enough for a small handful. Place all the open ends so they are facing the same direction.

Next, using the large twist or zip ties, tightly bundle the pieces together. Run the wire under each tie and twist the two ends together at the top to form a hanger. Finally, find a sheltered but bright location in your yard to hang the bundle, making sure that it is at least a few feet above the ground and all the stems are horizontal and level.

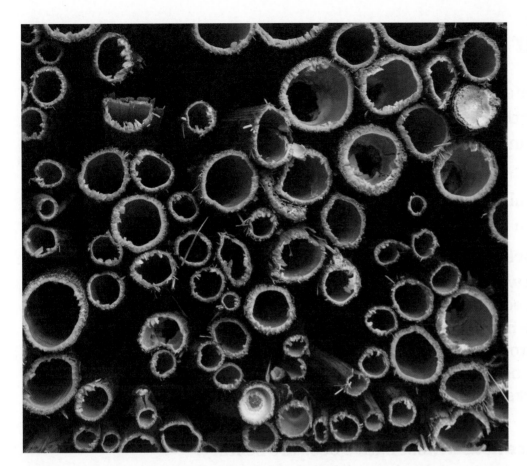

An example of how a bee bundle nest might look.

You can scatter several stem bundles throughout your yard. Be patient, as it may take some time for native bees to find your nest structure.

Make Your Yard Bug-friendly

Insects and other arthropods have pretty simple needs. Just like other organisms, they require food, shelter, and nesting sites or locations for their young.

You can help give insects a good home. Just a few simple steps are all you need to take to make your yard bug-friendly:

1. Make a log or rock pile. Log or rock piles create great hiding places, overwintering spots, food, and homes for many different insects and other arthropods. To make a simple log or stone habitat, simply stack logs or rocks of different sizes on top of each other. Your pile can be large or small, messy or neat, it really doesn't matter. Just make sure the wood/rocks you use are from your yard/area. The bugs will benefit.

2. Build a native bee house. Most native bees are solitary. They either nest in the ground or in cavities. A native bee house (see page 92) will help provide important nesting sites for these beneficial insects.

3. Plant a container garden for pollinators. Even small spaces can make a difference. Simply include 3-5 different flowering plants in a large pot. For best results, include plants with flowers of different colors, shapes, and sizes. They will help provide food in the form of nectar and pollen for hungry pollinators. For an added benefit, include a butterfly host plant. Host plants provide food for hungry caterpillars. Some good choices are milkweed, fennel, and parsley.

4. Avoid pesticides. Pesticides are chemicals designed to kill insects, particularly pests. However, many are broad-spectrum, which means they also often kill other beneficial or "good" bugs.

Gardening for Bugs:
Plant Native Plants

It's easy to garden for bugs. Many insects benefit from plants in the landscape. Plants provide food, shelter, nesting sites, and even homes for insects. Not all plants are created equal. Some, especially introduced or non-native species, provide few resources for insects, while others offer a lot.

Native plants are the best options for insects. Native plants are those that naturally occur in the area where you live. As a result, they are used to the local conditions such as temperature, rainfall, and soil, and the insects in the area have adapted to depend on them. They also generally offer many more benefits to a greater number of different insects than non-native plants. For example, butterfly caterpillars primarily feed on native plants.

Here is a list of familiar, sought-after insects and the native plants they depend on. If you want to attract them, planting these native plants is a good start!

Sunflowers attracts bees and other pollinators. They are found all over the United States.

Blazing Star attracts bees, butterflies, and moths. It is found all over the United States.

California Poppies attract bees. They are found in the western region of the United States.

Bee Balm attracts bees, butterflies, and moths. It is found all over the United States.

Aster attracts bees, butterflies, wasps, flies, beetles, and moths. It is found all over the United States.

Spiderwort attracts bees, butterflies, wasps, flies, and moths. It is found in the eastern region of the United States.

Wild Indigo attracts bees. It is found in the eastern region of the United States.

Milkweed attracts Monarch Butterflies and Caterpillars, plus many other insects. It is found found all over the United States.

Black-eyed Susans attract bees, butterflies, and other pollinators. They are found all over the United States.

Purple Coneflowers attract bees, butterflies, and moths. They are found in the western and central regions of the United States.

Salvia attracts bees and other pollinators. It is found all over the United States.

Coreopsis attracts bees, beetles, butterflies, wasps, flies, and moths. It is found all over the United States.

Goldenrod attracts bees, butterflies, wasps, flies, beetles, and moths. It is found all over the United States.

Ironweed attracts butterflies and other pollinators. It is found in the eastern and central regions of the United States.

Gardening for Bugs: Five Easy Plants to Help Welcome Bugs

While native plants are best for bugs, many easy-to-find plants are also good options. They can help make your yard more welcoming by providing resources to butterflies, bees, beetles, and many other cool critters. Better yet, they can also be easily grown from seed in a container, in a flower bed, or mixed into bare patches in a yard area.

Here is a list of easy-to-find and easy-to-grow plants that are great for bugs:

Cornflower is a great nectar and pollen source for bees, butterflies, and other pollinators.

Zinnia is a great nectar and pollen source for bees, butterflies, and other pollinators.

Clover provides food and habitat for insects.

Dill attracts many beneficial insects such as Green Lacewings and small wasps. It also provides food for Black Swallowtail and Anise Swallowtail Caterpillars.

Cosmos are a great nectar and pollen source for bees, butterflies, and other pollinators.

Community Science and Ways to Learn More

Technology offers many great tools to help you learn and explore the outdoor world. There are many apps and websites that enable anyone with curiosity and a phone camera to contribute to community science. Here is a rundown of a few fun, kid-friendly projects:

iNaturalist: *www.inaturalist.org/pages/seek_app*
The Seek App by iNaturalist is perfect for young naturalists and their families and can be used on a smartphone or tablet. It uses the camera on your device and image recognition to help identify insects, plants, and other organisms that you encounter. It can also help you learn more about what you find, and users even earn badges in the process!

The Lost Ladybug Project: *www.lostladybug.org*
Although these familiar insects are called ladybugs, these small insects are actually beetles. They are a diverse group of insects with nearly 500 different species found in North America. While ladybugs tend to be small, round, and are often orange or red in color with some combination of black spots, their exact appearance varies quite a bit by species.

Most ladybugs are considered "good bugs." As adults and larvae, they are hungry predators, feeding on other small insects, including many common plant pests such as aphids. Unfortunately, ladybug populations are declining, with some once-common species becoming quite rare. The Lost Ladybug Project is trying to better understand what is happening and why—and they need your help.

Note for parents: Seek is kid-safe and fun for families; there is no registration involved, and no user data is collected.

Convergent Lady Beetle

It's fun and simple to participate. Just complete a few easy steps:

1. Go outside and find some ladybugs. Follow the simple instructions provided by the Lost Ladybug Project.

2. When you find a ladybug—photograph it!

3. With the help of an adult, upload your digital images using the Lost Ladybug submission form, along with the time, date, location, and habitat (e.g. garden, wild field, or corn field).

Congratulations, you are now a community scientist! The photos and information you provide can be used by researchers to help prevent more ladybugs from declining.

Bumble Bee Watch: *www.bumblebeewatch.org* Bumblebees are large, plump insects best known for their fuzzy, black-and-yellow bodies. They are common flower visitors and highly beneficial pollinators. Of the 46 different species that occur in the United States and Canada, the populations of many are declining. Bumble Bee Watch is a program designed to track and conserve North America's bumblebees. It relies on information collected by community scientists, and you can help.

It's the perfect project to do with your parents, teachers, or with the whole family. The first step is to go outside and look for bumblebees. You can do this in your yard, a nearby field or park, or even on your next vacation. Because bumblebees are pollinators, they are often easily spotted at flowers. When you see one, snap a picture with your camera, smartphone, or tablet. Then, with the help of your parents or teacher, upload your bumblebee photos on the project website to start a virtual bumblebee collection. You can use the great resources provided to help identify the species you photographed and have them verified by an expert entomologist. You can also learn about bumblebees, their ecology, and ongoing conservation efforts to help protect them—and even see what other people have spotted. It's a fun way to record your observations and help scientists in the process.

Community Science and Ways to Learn More

Field Guides are books designed to help you identify the insects and other wildlife that you see. They are the perfect companion for a field trip, hike, or any outdoor adventure. Field guides provide pictures of individual species and information such as identifying characteristics, range, and habitat—as well as other fun facts. While there are many field guides to choose from, here are some to consider:

Eaton, E. and Kaufman, K. *Kaufman Field Guide to Insects of North America.* New York: Houghton Mifflin Co, 2007.

Evans, A. *National Geographic Backyard Guide to Insects and Spiders of North America.* Washington, D.C.: National Geographic, 2017.

Evans, A. *National Wildlife Federation Field Guide to Insects and Spiders & Related Species of North America.* New York: Sterling Pub, 2008.

Phillips, D. *Insects of North America: A Field Guide to Over 300 Insects.* Guliford: Falcon, 2019.

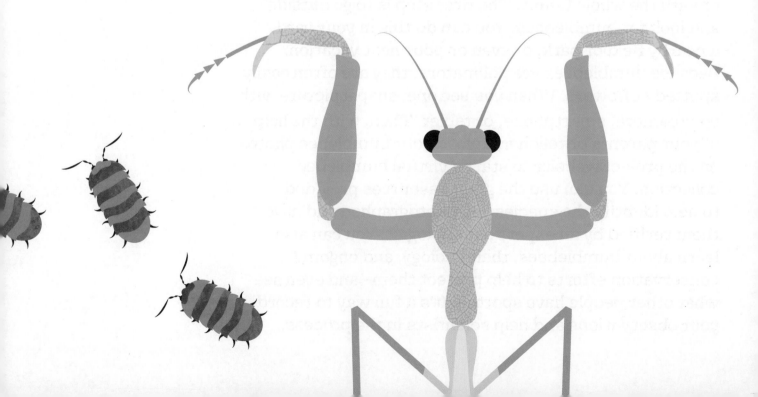

Activity & Quiz Answers

Page 13, Activity: Label the Parts of the House Fly: 1. Head 2. Compound Eyes 3. Thorax 4. Legs 5. Abdomen

Page 13, Quiz Time: 1. 2 2. 4

Page 17, Activity: Insect—or Not?: Insects: 2, 5, 7, 8, 11, and 12

Page 25, Activity: Bee, Wasp, or Ant Challenge: 1. Wasp 2. Wasp 3. Bee 4. Wasp 5. Ant 6. Bee 7. Wasp 8. Bee 9. Ant

Page 32, Quiz Time: 1. C. House Fly 2. D. In water

Page 35, Quiz Time: 1. D. 11 inches

Page 44, Activity: Native or Non-native?: 1. Native 2. Non-native 3. Non-native 4. Non-native 5. Non-native 6. Non-native 7. Non-native 8. Native 9. Native 10. Non-native Bonus: 2, 4, 5, 6, 7, 10 are all Invasive

Page 70, Activity: Which Insects Can Sting?: 1, 2, and 6 can sting

Page 71, Activity: Which Insects Taste Bad: 1, 2, and 3 taste bad

Glossary

Abdomen: The last and usually the longest or largest section of an insect's body. It contains the reproductive, digestive, and excretory systems.

Arthropods: An invertebrate animal that has an external skeleton, a segmented body, and jointed appendages such as legs and antennae.

Complete Metamorphosis: The process by which insects that pass through four distinct stages when developing: egg, larva, pupa, and adult. (Butterflies are an example.)

Entomology: The scientific study of insects.

Exoskeleton: An insect's hard (or generally hard) outer body covering, which provides protection and support.

Head: The first of three main sections on an insect's body, consisting of eyes, mouthparts, and two segmented antennae.

Herbivores: Organisms that feed on plants.

Incomplete Metamorphosis: The process by which insects that pass through three distinct stages when developing: egg, nymph, and adult. (Grasshoppers are an example.)

Insects: The largest and most diverse group of arthropods. They can be separated from other arthropods by having a three-part body consisting of a head, thorax, and abdomen.

Osmeterium: A bad-smelling forked organ that swallowtail caterpillars can use to defend themselves.

Parasitoids: Organisms that live in or attach to the bodies of other organisms, primarily insects and arthropods, eventually killing them.

Predators: Organisms that capture and feed on other organisms.

Glossary

Proboscis: The long, tongue-like mouthparts of an insect. These mouthparts are typically found in butterflies and moths and are used for sipping liquid food, such as flower nectar.

Spiracles: A series of small holes along the sides of an insect's body, which it uses to breathe.

Thorax: The second of three main sections of an insect's body. The thorax supports structures that enable the insect to move; these structures include three pairs of legs and one or two pairs of wings.

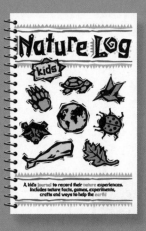
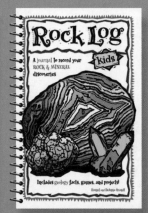
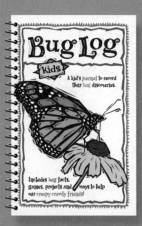

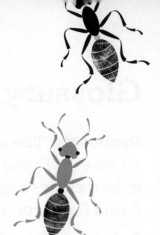

Bug Bingo

Test your bug knowledge with a game of Bingo!

Have an adult help you cut out the following four pages so that you and your friends can go on a Bingo hunt for beetles, butterflies, praying mantises, and more! Here's how it works:

Look for examples from the most-common and familiar orders of insects noted in each square. When you find one, cross out the square with an X or color it in. Keep searching for the things in the squares until you've made a row, column, or diagonal line of 5 connected squares.

Take note that the center square is a free space! Everyone gets that square.

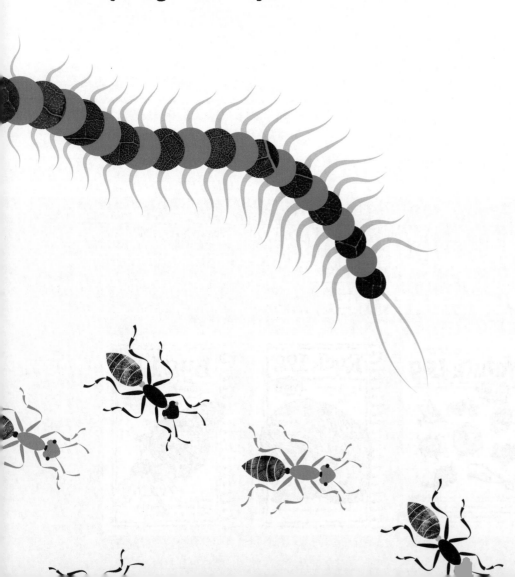

BINGO

Soldier Beetle Order Coleoptera	**Tersa Sphinx Moth** Order Lepidoptera	**Mourning Cloak Butterfly** Order Lepidoptera	**Water Strider** Order Hemiptera	**Carpenter Ant** Order Hymenoptera
Eastern Tiger Swallowtail Order Lepidoptera	**Fall Field Cricket** Order Orthoptera	**Robber Fly** Order Diptera	**Giant Water Bug** Order Hemiptera	**Ladybug** Order Coleoptera
Cockroach Order Blattodea	**Firefly** Order Coleoptera	**FREE SPACE**	**Leafhopper** Order Hemiptera	**Bumblebee** Order Hymenoptera
Paper Wasp Order Hymenoptera	**Earwig** Order Dermaptera	**Lubber Grasshopper** Order Orthoptera	**Pond Damselfly** Order Odonata	**Green Lacewing** Order Neuroptera
Mayfly Order Ephemeroptera	**Walking Stick** Order Phasmida	**Crane Fly** Order Diptera	**Cicada** Order Hemiptera	**Praying Mantis** Order Mantodea

Sketch, Measure, and Describe What You Find #1

Scientists record their observations, as it makes their findings easier to study (and to share with other scientists). Use the blank page below to sketch some of the neat bugs you find. To help make them easier to draw, you may wish to temporarily capture them in a clear plastic jar. This way, you can closely observe an organism without it getting away.

Use the ruler on the bottom of this page to measure their size. Then, for each bug, describe them in more detail. Record their color, where you found them, the time of year, and any unique features. Scientists use information (data) like this to help study species and determine what they are. Once you have finished, use a field guide to see if you can determine what kind of insect you saw. You may even be able to identify the particular species!

Description
Size, date, location, temperature, order, etc.

_____

_____

_____

_____

_____

_____

_____

_____

Sketch

¼ ½ ¾ |1 |2 |3 |4 |5 |6 |7 |8

BINGO

Pond Damselfly Order Odonata	**Carpenter Ant** Order Hymenoptera	**Crane Fly** Order Diptera	**Mourning Cloak Butterfly** Order Lepidoptera	**Cicada** Order Hemiptera
Praying Mantis Order Mantodea	**Lubber Grasshopper** Order Orthoptera	**Eastern Tiger Swallowtail** Order Lepidoptera	**Mayfly** Order Ephemeroptera	**Paper Wasp** Order Hymenoptera
Green Lacewing Order Neuroptera	**Firefly** Order Coleoptera	**FREE SPACE**	**Leafhopper** Order Hemiptera	**Bumblebee** Order Hymenoptera
Earwig Order Dermaptera	**Cockroach** Order Blattodea	**Tersa Sphinx Moth** Order Lepidoptera	**Giant Water Bug** Order Hemiptera	**Robber Fly** Order Diptera
Soldier Beetle Order Coleoptera	**Walking Stick** Order Phasmida	**Water Strider** Order Hemiptera	**Fall Field Cricket** Order Orthoptera	**Ladybug** Order Coleoptera

Sketch, Measure, and Describe What You Find #2

Scientists record their observations, as it makes their findings easier to study (and to share with other scientists). Use the blank page below to sketch some of the neat bugs you find. To help make them easier to draw, you may wish to temporarily capture them in a clear plastic jar. This way, you can closely observe an organism without it getting away.

Use the ruler on the bottom of this page to measure their size. Then, for each bug, describe them in more detail. Record their color, where you found them, the time of year, and any unique features. Scientists use information (data) like this to help study species and determine what they are. Once you have finished, use a field guide to see if you can determine what kind of insect you saw. You may even be able to identify the particular species!

Description
Size, date, location, temperature, order, etc.

_____

_____

_____

_____

_____

_____

_____

_____

Sketch

¼ ½ ¾ |1 |2 |3 |4 |5 |6 |7 |8

BINGO

B	I	N	G	O
Earwig Order Dermaptera	**Paper Wasp** Order Hymenoptera	**Fall Field Cricket** Order Orthoptera	**Mayfly** Order Ephemeroptera	**Robber Fly** Order Diptera
Eastern Tiger Swallowtail Order Lepidoptera	**Mourning Cloak Butterfly** Order Lepidoptera	**Lubber Grasshopper** Order Orthoptera	**Firefly** Order Coleoptera	**Giant Water Bug** Order Hemiptera
Cockroach Order Blattodea	**Soldier Beetle** Order Coleoptera	**FREE SPACE**	**Leafhopper** Order Hemiptera	**Carpenter Ant** Order Hymenoptera
Tersa Sphinx Moth Order Lepidoptera	**Pond Damselfly** Order Odonata	**Bumblebee** Order Hymenoptera	**Ladybug** Order Coleoptera	**Praying Mantis** Order Mantodea
Water Strider Order Hemiptera	**Walking Stick** Order Phasmida	**Cicada** Order Hemiptera	**Crane Fly** Order Diptera	**Green Lacewing** Order Neuroptera

Sketch, Measure, and Describe What You Find #3

Scientists record their observations, as it makes their findings easier to study (and to share with other scientists). Use the blank page below to sketch some of the neat bugs you find. To help make them easier to draw, you may wish to temporarily capture them in a clear plastic jar. This way, you can closely observe an organism without it getting away.

Use the ruler on the bottom of this page to measure their size. Then, for each bug, describe them in more detail. Record their color, where you found them, the time of year, and any unique features. Scientists use information (data) like this to help study species and determine what they are. Once you have finished, use a field guide to see if you can determine what kind of insect you saw. You may even be able to identify the particular species!

Description
Size, date, location, temperature, order, etc.

_____

_____

_____

_____

_____

_____

_____

_____

Sketch

¼ ½ ¾ |1 |2 |3 |4 |5 |6 |7 |8

BINGO

Giant Water Bug Order Hemiptera	**Tersa Sphinx Moth** Order Lepidoptera	**Crane Fly** Order Diptera	**Water Strider** Order Hemiptera	**Lubber Grasshopper** Order Orthoptera
Praying Mantis Order Mantodea	**Cicada** Order Hemiptera	**Robber Fly** Order Diptera	**Soldier Beetle** Order Coleoptera	**Earwig** Order Dermaptera
Green Lacewing Order Neuroptera	**Firefly** Order Coleoptera	**FREE SPACE**	**Leafhopper** Order Hemiptera	**Bumblebee** Order Hymenoptera
Paper Wasp Order Hymenoptera	**Ladybug** Order Coleoptera	**Carpenter Ant** Order Hymenoptera	**Pond Damselfly** Order Odonata	**Eastern Tiger Swallowtail** Order Lepidoptera
Mayfly Order Ephemeroptera	**Walking Stick** Order Phasmida	**Mourning Cloak Butterfly** Order Lepidoptera	**Fall Field Cricket** Order Orthoptera	**Cockroach** Order Blattodea

Sketch, Measure, and Describe What You Find #4

Scientists record their observations, as it makes their findings easier to study (and to share with other scientists). Use the blank page below to sketch some of the neat bugs you find. To help make them easier to draw, you may wish to temporarily capture them in a clear plastic jar. This way, you can closely observe an organism without it getting away.

Use the ruler on the bottom of this page to measure their size. Then, for each bug, describe them in more detail. Record their color, where you found them, the time of year, and any unique features. Scientists use information (data) like this to help study species and determine what they are. Once you have finished, use a field guide to see if you can determine what kind of insect you saw. You may even be able to identify the particular species!

Description
Size, date, location, temperature, order, etc.

_____

_____

_____

_____

_____

_____

_____

_____

Sketch

¼ ½ ¾ 1 2 3 4 5 6 7 8

Recommended Reading

Daniels, Jaret. *Insects & Bugs of North America: Your Way to Easily Identify Insects & Bugs* (Adventure Quick Guides). Cambridge, Minnesota: Adventure Publications, 2019.

Daniels, Jaret. *Backyard Bugs: An Identification Guide to Common Insects, Spiders, and More.* Cambridge, Minnesota: Adventure Publications, 2017.

Daniels, Jaret. *Butterflies of the Northeast: Identify Butterflies with Ease* (Adventure Quick Guides). Cambridge, Minnesota: Adventure Publications, 2019.

Daniels, Jaret. *Butterflies of the Northwest: Your Way to Easily Identify Butterflies* (Adventure Quick Guides). Cambridge, Minnesota: Adventure Publications, 2020.

Daniels, Jaret. *Butterflies of the Midwest: Identify Butterflies with Ease* (Adventure Quick Guides). Cambridge, Minnesota: Adventure Publications, 2016.

Websites

Seek by iNaturalist (www.inaturalist.org/pages/seek_app): This application uses the camera on your smartphone or tablet, along with image recognition, to help you identify insects, plants, and other organisms.

BugGuide. (www.bugguide.net/node/view/15740): An online resource providing identification, images, and information on insects, spiders, and their relatives for the United States and Canada.

Butterflies and Moths of North America. (www.butterfliesandmoths.org): An online resource providing information, images, and occurrence data for butterflies and moths.

Photo Credits

Cover and Interior Illustrations by Fallon Venable

All images copyright by their prospective photographers.
Brett Ortler: 15 (top), 22 (wasp), 23 (crane fly), 33 (egg),52, 53 (ants), 53 (earthworm), 53 (beetle), 55 (ambush bugs, bees, beetles, butterflies, flies), 62 (craneflies), 62 (beetles), 65 (beetles and walking sticks), 75, 76, 83 (all), 85, 87, 99; **CDC/James Gathany:** 57 (mosquito larvae); and **Jaret Daniels:** 120 (author photo).

Images used under license from Shutterstock:
Lost_in_the_Midwest: 73 (top); **abcphotosystem:** 57 (water striders); **Achkin:** 35 and 62 (mayflies); **Adam Tremel:** 18 (odonata), 21 (twelve-spotted skimmer dragonfly); **Akvals:** 18 (hemiptera), 27 (dog-day cicada); **Aleksandar Grozdanovski:** 16 (snail); **Alex Staroseltsev:** 19 (lady beetle); **Alice Day:** 12 (bottom left); **Amelia Martin:** 59 (ants); **an_nature_photography:** 25 (4); **Anatolich:** 57 (dragonfly nymphs); **AndrewASkolnick:** 57 (giant water bug); **Anest:** 53 (centipede); **Ankor Light:** 27 (woolly aphid); **annop youngrot:** 18 (diptera), 23 (house fly); **Anton Kozyrev:** 19 (colorado potato beetle), 34 (green stink bug); **Apostle:** 98 (bottom left); **ArtEvent ET:** 60 (earwig); **ashok india:** 60 (millipede); **Auhustsinovich:** 100 (top left); **Ben Petcharapiracht:** 98 (middle left); **Bildagentur Zoonar GmbH:** 70 (3); **Bill Kennedy:** 27 (red-banded leafhopper); **Bill Kennedy:** 59 (boxelder bugs); **BOb Pool:** 17 (pillbug); **Breck P. Kent:** 31 (chrysalis); **Brenda McGee-Paap:** 63; **Brian Lasenby:** 18 (phasmida), 26 and 34 (walking stick); **Butterfly Hunter:** 17 (butterfly); **ButtermilkgirlVirginia:** 62 (praying mantis); **Cameramannz:** 35 (caterpillar); **Cathy Keifer:** 35 (polyphemus moth); **Charlie Floyd:** 45 (8); **Christian Buch:** 23 and 35 (green bottle fly); **Christian Ouellet:** 18 (orthoptera), 24 (lubber grasshopper); **Cindy Creighton:** 18 (ephemeroptera), 28, 37, and 39 (mayfly); **Conrad Barrington:** 31 (larva), 59 (centipedes), 79 (right); **crystalt-mc:** 17 (millipede); **D. Kucharski K. Kucharska:** 45 (6); **Daniel Prudek:** 43 (bottom left), 70 (2); **Danut Vieru:** 12 (top center); **Dark Egg:** 23 (hover fly); **David Byron Keener:** 71 (5); **dba87:** 16 (pillbug); **Deep Desert Photography:** 47; **DeRebus:** 45 (4); **Diane N. Ennis:** 24 (carolina grasshopper); **DJTaylor:** 62 (moths); **Dmitry Demkin:** 96 (left); **DONGSEUN YANG:** 57 (diving beetles); **Doug Lemke:** 34 (dragonfly); **Dr.MYM:** 12 (bottom right); **Dustin Rhoades:** 11 (top left); **Eddie Gibson:** 12 (top left); **Eddie Phantana:** 59 (termites); **edstines:** 61 (orb-weaving spider); **Elliotte Rusty Harold:** 17 (beetle), 19 (eastern firefly); 22 (bumblebee); 35 (ant); 70 (7); **Ernie Cooper:** 8 (crustaceans); 57 (water boatmen); 65 (katydids); **Evgeny Haritonov:** 93; **Federico Crovetto:** 14 (top); 60 (jumping spiders); **Fotema:** 58; **Frances van der Merwe:** 35 (aphid); **frank60:** 45 (10); **Frauenversand Cleopatra:** 53 (earwig); **gabrielmcg021:** 37 and 39 (monarch butterfly), 71 (2); **gan chaonan:** 60 (cockroach); **Georges_Creations:** 65 (praying mantis); **Ger Bosma Photos:** 43 (top left); 45 (2); **Gerry Bishop:** 11 (top center), 33 (nymph); **guentermanaus:** 18 (blattodea); 26 and 53 (cockroach); **GypsyPictureShow:** 74; **haireena:** 101; **Henri Koskinen:** 18 (dermaptera); 28 (earwig); 62 (green lacewing); **Henrik Larsson:** 17 and 55 (spider); **Herman Wong HM:** 44, 45 (7); **HHelene:** 34 (earwig); **High Mountain:** 97 (middle right); **Ian Grainger:** 27 (shield bug); **Igor Nikushin:** 60 (centipede); **Ihor Hvozdetskyi:** 43 (middle right), 45 (5), 65 (spiders); **Ingrid CH:** 11 (bottom); **irin-k:** 13; **J Gillispie:** 65 (caterpillars); **J.J. Gouin:** 61 (paper wasp nest); **James W. Thompson:** 71 (1); **Jason Patrick Ross:** 35 (orange sulfer butterfly); **Jay Ondreicka:** 53 (sowbug);

Jennifer Bosvert: 25 (8); **JGade:** 17 (leafhopper); **Jim and Lynne Weber:** 45 (1); **John Bradford:** 61 (moth caterpillars); **Josef Stemeseder:** 71 (4); **ju_see:** 9; **Julian Popov:** 98 (bottom right); **K E Magoon:** 97 (top left); **kallen1979:** 70 (1); **Kelly Marken:** 23 (halteres on crane fly); **Kendall Wiggins:** 55 (praying mantis); **Kent Sievers:** 43 (top right); **Kevin Collison:** 18 (lepidoptera), 20 (giant swallowtail butterfly); **Kira Immordino:** 97 (bottom left); **Kras_Stock:** 22 (ant); **Kwanbenz:** 100 (bottom right); **kzww:** 17 (earthworm); **Laura Dinraths:** 16 (slug); **Leena Robinson:** 31 (pupa), 100 (bottom left); **LegART:** 59 (bark beetle); **Maarten Zeehandelaar:** 95; **Maciej Olszewski:** 25 (7); **Macronatura.es:** 60 (silverfish); **MakroBetz:** 7; **Malachi Jacobs:** 34 (red-legged grasshopper); **Maple Ferryman:** 24 (fork-tailed bush katydid); **Marek Mierzejewski:** 20 (mourning cloak butterfly); **Marek Mnich:** 35 (green lacewing); **Martina Simonazzi:** 57 (backswimmers); **Mary Terriberry:** 91; **Matee Nuserm:** 17 (grasshopper); **Matt Benoit:** 45 (9); **Matt Jeppson:** 20 (cecropia moth), 36 and 39 (luna moth); **Maxim Novikov:** 59 (spiders); **McGraw:** 98 (middle right); **Media Marketing:** 51; **Melinda Fawver:** 17 (carpenter ant), 20 (tersa sphinx moth); 62 (antlion); **melissamn:** 67; **Michael Siluk:** 16 (sowbug); **Michael Siluk:** 21 (tule bluet damselfly); **Michal Ziemski:** 59 (earwig); **Micheal Benard:** 23 (robber fly); **NadyGinzburg:** 73 (bottom); **Napat:** 81; **Napat_M:** 60 (house flies); **Natalia Kuzmina:** 56; **Nataliia Yankovets:** 49; **natmac stock:** 21 (meadowhawk dragonfly); **Naxim Nikiforov:** 11 (top right); **newsony:** 61 (ant nest); **Nina B:** 97 (bottom right); **Nopparat:** 100 (top middle); **NOTE OMG:** 42 (left); **Ondrej Prosicky:** 8 (hexapods); **Paul Brennan:** 98 (top right); **Paul Reeves Photography:** 12 (bottom right), 18 (hymenoptera and coleoptera), 19 (six-spotted tiger beetle); 21 (damselfly perching and sedge sprite damselfly), 22 (yellowjacket), 24 (fall field cricket), 25 (1, 2, and 3), 37 (banded woolybear), 39 (banded woolybear), 42 (right), 54 (top); 55 (day-flying moths and wasps), 59 (carpenter bee and wood wasp), 69 (all), 70 (6 and 8), 89; **Paul Sparks:** 43 (bottom right), 45 (3), 70 (4); **Pavel Krasensky:** 17 (wasp); **photographyfirm:** 15 (bottom); **prasom boonpong:** 17 (centipede); **Protasov AN:** 6, 43 (middle left); **Puttachat Kumkrong:** 8 (myriapods); **Rabbitti:** 30 (adult); **Randy R:** 35 (milkweed bug); **RattiyaThongdumhyu:** 79 (left); **RomBo 64:** 37 and 39 (bumblebee), 100 (top right); **Ron Maxwell:** 32 (adult); **Ron Rowan Photography:** 8 (arachnids); **Rose Ludwig:** 21 (dragonfly perching); **Russell Marshall:** 25 (5); **Sacha Ye Gauthier:** 70 (5); **samray:** 55 (robber fly); **Sari ONeal:** 34 (white-lined sphinx moth), 71 (3); **Serguei Koultchitskii:** 34 (giant swallowtail); **Silent Shoot:** 27 (milkweed assassin bug); **Steve Bower:** 18 (mantodea), 29; **StudioNewmarket:** 35, 36 and 38 (june bug); **SunflowerMomma:** 102; **Susan Schmitz:** 17 (scorpion); **Suzanne Tucker:** 37 and 38 (firefly), 86; **tea maeklong:** 26 (termites); **TechnoSavage:** 54 (bottom); **The Downeast Artisan:** 97 (middle left); **TheLazyPineapple:** 65 (grasshoppers); **T-I:** 64; **Tom Franks:** 14 (bottom); **tome213:** 53 (spider); **tviolet:** 97 (top right); **Viktoriya A:** 98 (top left); **Vinicius R. Souza:** 34 (lady beetle); **Vitalii Hulai:** 32 (bottom); **Vitolga:** 57 (whirligig beetles); **watchara panyajun:** 35 (cockroach); **Wirestock Creators:** 25 (6); **wjarek:** 96 (right); **wnarong:** 25 (9); and **yanikap:** 12 (top right).

About the Author

Jaret C. Daniels, Ph.D., is a professional nature photographer, author, native plant enthusiast, and entomologist at the University of Florida, specializing in insect ecology and conservation.

He has authored numerous scientific papers, popular articles, and books on gardening, wildlife conservation, insects, and butterflies, including butterfly field guides for Florida, Georgia, the Carolinas, Ohio, and Michigan. He is also coauthor of *Insects & Bugs for Kids: An Introduction to Entomology* and *Wildflowers of the Southeast Field Guide*.

Jaret currently lives in Gainesville, Florida, with his wife, Stephanie.

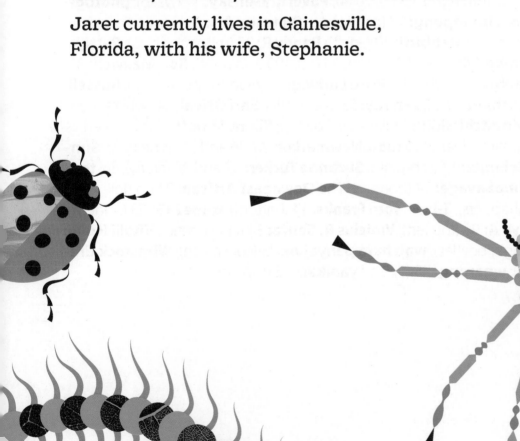